ANTIQUES ROADSHOW

WITH THE COMPLIMENTS OF

LYONS
ORIGINAL
Coffee

ANTIQUES ROADSHOW

○

TIARAS, TALLBOYS AND TEDDY BEARS

A SELECTION FROM THE
RADIO TIMES ANTIQUES
ROADSHOW COLUMN

Edited by
Christopher Lewis

With illustrations
by Rodney Shackell

BBC BOOKS

Published by BBC Books,
a division of BBC Enterprises Limited,
Woodlands, 80 Wood Lane, London W12 0TT

This collection first published in book form, 1991
© In the contributions, *Radio Times* 1989, 1990
© In this arrangement, BBC Books 1991

ISBN 0 563 36179 4

Designed by Peartree Design Associates
Illustrations © Rodney Shackell 1991

Set in Janson by Ace Filmsetting Ltd, Frome
Printed and bound in Great Britain by Clays Ltd, St Ives plc
Cover printed by Clays Ltd, St Ives plc

CONTENTS

INTRODUCTION

WITH HELPFUL ADVICE, strong opinion, amusing anecdote and gentle lessons in antiques and fine arts, the *Radio Times Antiques Roadshow* column has educated and entertained its readers. So much so that in a survey conducted by the magazine to enquire what parts of the magazine were most read, the Antiques column came near the top.

Did you know that Sir Henry Doulton made his fortune manufacturing the pipes that cured the nation's sewerage problem in the nineteenth century? That the Duke of Wellington had a larger-than-life marble statue of Napoleon in the entrance hall of Apsley House? That 'Ming' means in translation simply the sound that dragons make, like 'miaow' for cats?

Tips for collectors abound, from commemorative mugs to teapots to glass sugar crushers. And there are the stories of the best of the *Antiques Roadshow* 'finds' – the slipware owl from Northampton (which was subsequently sold for £20000); the four priceless Chinese cloisonné figures of Old Testament prophets which turned up in Sweden; and the unknown painting of a little girl by the Dadaist artist Schwitters, brought to the *Roadshow* by the subject herself, now a mature woman.

The two-thousand-year-old figure of an Egyptian servant guarding his master in the tomb, the dead Roman at the bottom of Henry Sandon's garden who had a taste for pots, make fascinating reading for historians and collectors alike. From Japanese and Chinese works of art, to musical boxes and Hornby train sets, this is a highly readable and informative collection of the best of the *Radio Times Antiques Roadshow* column.

CHRISTOPHER LEWIS
Executive Producer
Antiques Roadshow

LARGER-THAN-LIFE NAPOLEON

Eric Knowles

P LACE IN ORDER of popularity the following portrait figures produced by Victorian Staffordshire potters:

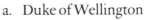

    a. Duke of Wellington
    b. Queen Victoria
    c. Napoleon Bonaparte.

If you are a regular player of the *Antiques Roadshow* game you may have a slight advantage. The answer, incredible though it may seem, is that Queen Victoria only manages a poor second, and then not to the Iron Duke, but to his famous adversary the Emperor Napoleon Bonaparte.

History books, so often quick to portray 'Old Boney' as the veritable anti-Christ, ignore the fact that many of the British concealed a real admiration for the Emperor. Even the Duke of Wellington himself displayed a definite respect for the man on at least one occasion. It was on the battlefield of Waterloo when the Duke and Napoleon came within sight and therefore range of each other. A young aide offered to attempt a shot at the Emperor with his pistol, only to be rebuked by the Duke who made it clear that the commanders of armies never made it their business to shoot at one another.

Whether in respect or admiration I know not, the Duke had a larger-than-life marble statue of Napoleon, in the guise of a classical warrior, erected in the entrance hall of Apsley House, his London abode. I am somehow unable to envisage Churchill keeping any form of effigy of Adolf Hitler – certainly not in such a prominent place, although in the Second World War chamber pots were produced decorated with Hitler's face and bearing the legend: 'Take a shot at old nasty'.

One of the earliest porcelain, as opposed to pottery, figures of the Emperor came from the famous South Yorkshire Rockingham factory. Produced in about 1832, the figure was possibly inspired by the sell-out drama and extravaganza *Napoleon Buonoparte* (sic) which opened at the Covent Garden Theatre in 1831. Incidentally, the inclusion of the letter U in the spelling of his name was not derived from the Italian spelling of the name (Buonaparte) but was an intentional form of ridicule on the part of the British.

The vast number of figures of Napoleon produced in Staffordshire varied in both quality and size, with most appearing to date between 1840 and 1860. They can generally be bought for less than £100. Most depict him standing in typical pose with arms folded or with one hand slipped into his waistcoat. Some were inspired by the illustrated covers of contemporary music sheets.

Several examples show the Emperor seated upon a rearing white charger and are obviously influenced by Jacques Louis David's painting, *Napoleon Crossing the Alps*, which now hangs in the Musée de Versailles. Monsieur David was granted a liberal slice of artistic licence by Napoleon who actually crossed the Alps not upon his magnificent white stallion, but seated astride a pack mule. But the Staffordshire potters did well out of 'Old Boney', and not one of them was prepared to portray him as a complete ass.

THE PRODUCTS OF WAR

Penny Brittain

THE STORMING OF THE BASTILLE in 1789, and the years of terror that followed, sent tremors throughout Europe. Then followed the Napoleonic Wars and the arrival in England of large numbers of French prisoners of war, fired by revolutionary ideas from their own country. There was genuine concern in Parliament that these prisoners posed a threat to the political stability of the country.

As a result reception centres were set up and condemned naval vessels were requisitioned and stripped to create floating 'hulks' moored in ports such as Plymouth and Chatham. New prisons were built on Dartmoor and at Norman Cross in Huntingdonshire. From 1797 for ten years Norman Cross was home for 6500 prisoners.

They were mostly conscripts, and many were skilled tradesmen. In the meagre conditions of prison they soon found need for extra rations and clothing and they began to make what we now know as prisoner of war work – objects created from the limited raw materials available from within the prison. Wood was used as a carcass material; it was overlaid with bone, straw and paper, and occasionally inlaid with precious materials such as copper and, very rarely, silver. The prisoners' rations included 5lb of meat a week, so bone, be it mutton or beef, was plentiful and could be augmented by an occasional foray to the prison kitchen.

The prisoners' talents were representative of many of the French craft guilds, and their skilled workmanship is apparent in the objects produced. The range was limited in the main to bone gaming boxes, models of French ships of the line, mechanical models of women spinning or churning butter and men sharpening knives. Straw work boxes were rarer, sometimes shaped as books and sometimes containing love tokens for their sweethearts. Occasionally a coquilla nut was carved. No two pieces are alike, and very few were signed or dated.

All the pieces are evocative. A letter in French found in a straw box reads:

> Joseph Dedoue, taken prisoner at the naval battle of Trafalgar, 21st October 1805, made this Box during the month of April 1814, and he hopes very much that it will be the last he will make in England for those brigands, scoundrels, abominable monsters the English who by their barbarous politics worthy only of cannibals, have held me nearly 10 years in their prison at Norman Cross, 26th April 1814.

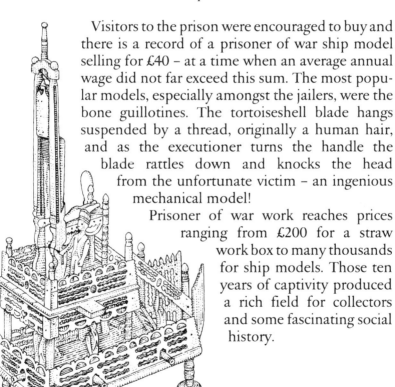

Visitors to the prison were encouraged to buy and there is a record of a prisoner of war ship model selling for £40 – at a time when an average annual wage did not far exceed this sum. The most popular models, especially amongst the jailers, were the bone guillotines. The tortoiseshell blade hangs suspended by a thread, originally a human hair, and as the executioner turns the handle the blade rattles down and knocks the head from the unfortunate victim – an ingenious mechanical model!

Prisoner of war work reaches prices ranging from £200 for a straw work box to many thousands for ship models. Those ten years of captivity produced a rich field for collectors and some fascinating social history.

COLLECTING LOCAL HISTORY

Terence Lockett

EVERYONE WANTS TO COLLECT something these days, but where do you start? I am often asked this, and in ceramics there is no single answer. If there were, we should all be collecting the same thing!

There is, however, one category of pottery or porcelain that seems to appeal to everyone and covers a wide price range – the local commemorative. Over thirty years ago I bought a Parian* porcelain bust of Richard Cobden MP, whose statue is a familiar landmark in St Peter's Square, Stockport. It was my first commemorative. My next, for a shilling, was a saucer printed with a picture of Stockport Sunday School, in its heyday the largest Sunday school in the world. Shortly afterwards, the building was demolished. So I had not simply bought a piece of the redundant crockery, but a piece of local history. There are literally thousands of similar pots which were made for a church, a Sunday school, even an hotel, or were produced to commemorate a special local event. For example, most co-operative societies commissioned plates depicting their premises to celebrate their diamond or golden jubilees. These no

---

* Parian – a type of porcelain resembling pure white marble from the Island of Paros. See page 68.

longer cost only a couple of pounds, but they are still good fun and not dear.

Some local commemoratives are both rare and expensive. A coronation mug made by Davenport with a portrait of Queen Victoria and the words 'Success to the Town and Trade of Preston' has been described as 'perhaps the rarest of all the Victorian coronation commemoratives'. Imagine my surprise when a lady produced a similar mug on a *Roadshow*, inscribed with the words 'Success to the Caledonian Free School Liverpool'. If the Preston mug is the rarest – I know of at least four of them – how rare is the Liverpool piece? Unique?

Mugs like this were regularly given to schoolchildren to celebrate coronations from the time of Queen Victoria onwards. In my own collection are the beakers given at the coronation of Edward VII to my mother and aunt by Brentnall Street Wesleyan Sunday School in Stockport in 1902. Most families have similar mementoes which are visually attractive, have personal associations and inform us of the history of our own locality.

In the period 1880–1914 German factories made porcelain pieces decorated with English views. With their bright pink borders they are very distinctive and collectable, but may not commemorate any specific event and are simply interesting tourist souvenirs. English manufacturers also made pots decorated with local views. Two I have 'picked up' are of the Monkey House at Belle Vue Zoo, now demolished, and the Pavilion Gardens at Buxton, happily still flourishing 120 years after they were opened.

Whether they commemorate places or people, these local items give an immediacy to a collection and can lead to fascinating research on local history. The Minton cup and saucer illustrated celebrates the coming of age of the son of the local worthy who once owned the ground upon which my house stands (not to mention half of this part of Cheshire). If you buy your local commemoratives away from your own locality they will usually be less expensive. They could be sound investments. Thirty years ago Cobden cost me £3. A fellow *Roadshow* expert told me the other day that it would fetch £250–300 at auction. No, it's not for sale. I liked him then and I still do. What better reason is there for buying an interesting piece?

EYE OF NEWT AND TOE OF FROG

Henry Sandon

I THINK IT WAS the buying of my first frog on the same day that I saw Shakespeare's *Macbeth* that did for me. My pot in my lap, I watched the three cackling witches casting their spells. What was it about frogs and newts in pots that has fascinated, frightened and amused people for so long?

For an enthusiastic collector of humorous English pottery, the best pieces are the frog mugs and loving cups made in the eighteenth and nineteenth centuries. They will usually have a poem on the outside and a modelled frog climbing up the inside, sometimes with a lizard as well. The finest collection of them was formed by Marjorie Davies, who bought her first mug in 1959 as a joke, became a fanatic and accumulated three hundred different examples, in her words 'transforming an idle interest into an addiction'. She gave the collection to the Stoke-on-Trent City Museum in 1987.

The origin of putting frogs (or toads) into beer mugs certainly goes back into the seventeenth century, as is testified by Samuel Pepys in his diary entry for 19 September 1666. He records a frolic played by a Mr Pinchbacke, who found a toad outside in the yard, popped it into his glass and drank from it without any harm. His friend Dr Goffe, who knew that sack would kill the toad, filled the pot up with strong drink and then refused a drink 'from a dead toad'.

The mugs were often known as ague mugs because it was thought that frogs and toads could cure ague. Toads have a rather bad reputation as the presumed familiar of witches and because they were thought to spit venom.

> A dark cave. In the middle, a cauldron boiling.
> *First Witch*: Toad, that under the cold stone,
> Days and nights hast thirty-one
> Swelter'd venom sleeping got,
> Boil thou first i' the charmed pot!

Also thrown in are eye of newt and toe of frog, not to mention a lizard's leg. How the audience at the Globe Theatre must have wriggled with fear! Much the same thoughts must have been in the minds of contemporary drinkers at the sight of these creatures in their mugs. Imagine the shock of a frog appearing through your drink, ready to jump down your throat.

The poems on the outside attempt to lessen the shock with such words as

> Though malt and venom seem united
> Don't break my pot or be affrighted
> For when it's full no spleen is seen
> And when it's empty it's quite clean.

The poem is almost up to Shakespeare's witches' standard. So don't be frightened by the creatures in the mug. As one version of the poem says,

> Whatever in this pot you see
> Don't throw it down to injure me.

When some of the creatures have mouth agape and spit beer at you as you drink, just put it down to the sense of fun there must have been in pubs of old, full of amiable drunks attempting to drink from puzzle jugs, fuddling cups and frog mugs. A far cry from the modern image of the lager lout.

BE MY VALENTINE

Victoria Leatham

LOVE TOKENS WERE very popular in Victorian times. In the nineteenth century you might have been fortunate enough to receive from your best beloved the gift of a sperm whale's tooth, nicely engraved – just what every girl needed. If this wasn't enough he might have gone the whole hog and carved a stay busk for your corset . . . what price romance today!

Stay busks were known in the days of Queen Elizabeth I, but the carving of scrimshaw, whales' teeth, walrus tusks and bone reached its heyday during the Victorian years. Sailors driven to desperation by long, tedious voyages could busy themselves making something for sale or to give to the object of their desire. These pieces, especially if of American origin, can command big money in the salerooms. You would expect to pay well over £1000 for a good pair of sperm whale teeth, but beware of bargains. Fakes abound.

The ability of the Victorians to trivialise a worthy sentiment has never been bettered than when it was applied to romance,

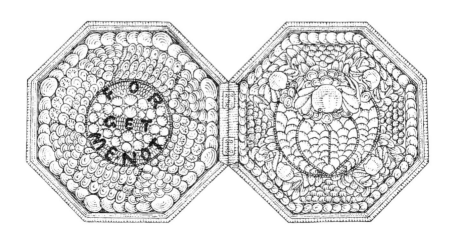

and romantic jewellery in particular. There was a vast industry manufacturing thousands of brooches decorated with doves, clasped hands, hearts pierced by arrows and so on. They even did a nice line in brooches and lockets with hair inside (somehow hair is just bearable when safely under glass). In fact, this Victorian sentimental jewellery is a good hunting ground for the collector; much of it is reasonably priced and it is infinitely nicer than modern reproductions.

Cast in a larger mould altogether was a group of items called shell valentines. These are attractive panels, usually octagonal, made of coloured paper on which hundreds of exotic shells have been stuck in a pattern. They were brought back to England from the West Indies in fair numbers during the nineteenth century. At one *Antiques Roadshow* in Glenrothes, Fife, a gentleman brought one of these to our 'Miscellaneous' table for appraisal. He knew all its history as it had been given to his grandmother by his grandfather when they were courting. She was captivated by her Valentine, and in the best romantic tradition married and lived happily ever after. The example I saw in Fife was valued for insurance at £600.

Part of the pleasure I get from discussing antiques with their owners is the wealth of stories attached to the items, romantic or otherwise. I was once valuing the contents of a house in a small country town. The owner was a young man whose father had recently passed away. As we worked through the contents of the sitting room, he was insistent that I should value the contents of a drawer in the bureau. On opening it I was confronted with the most menacing collection of old teeth I have ever seen. He explained that he needed the gold fillings valued so that he could assess their suitability as a potential wedding ring for his fiancée. I declined the invitation! The macabre side of the Victorians is alive and well today.

TIARA BOOM DAYS

Geoffrey Munn

'THE QUEEN HAS TAKEN the trouble to wear a tiara – why have you not?' was the curt rebuke of King Edward VII to a lady who had assumed that an enormous diamond crescent in the hair would do as well.

Always a symbol of rank, tiaras are not, as is commonly supposed, the preserve of royalty alone. They date back to the very beginnings of human civilisation and are a reference to triumphal garlands of flowers and leaves worn by the victorious in war as well as by the winners of musical and athletic contests. Soon the sprays of natural ornament were simulated by hammered gold and silver, and as time went by, every form of decoration was lavished upon them. From the eighteenth century onwards the form and ancient meaning of these, the most poetic and flattering of all jewels, was sometimes lost in a scintillating display of the finest precious stones. However, a vestigial reference to the ancient function and design of the tiara always remains in the form of a pair of open loops at the back from which ribbons are tied. By these they are distinguished from coronets.

Today there is hardly a gathering where tiaras can be worn, and hardly ever are they mandatory. Thanks to television, one such mandatory gathering is open to the public gaze – the State Opening of Parliament. In the past, when a higher percentage of the Upper House was made up of hereditary noblemen, the wife of each would be equipped with one of the family jewels. But the granting of life peerages to those without ancestral gems sets them an awkward problem, so rare have tiaras become.

Very often a head ornament of this nature will be designed for more than one purpose. Sometimes a diamond fringe tiara can, with the help of a minute set of gold tools, be taken off its frame to make an articulated (flexible) necklace. A garland of diamond flowers may, for instance, be taken apart to form several brooches. The pearls which hang in the loops of the nineteenth-century Russian tiara worn by the Queen can be substituted for emerald drops by a very simple process. Unfortunately those tiaras which are any less versatile are greatly at risk of being broken up for the stones which they contain. These are then recut and polished to make more modest and invariably less attractive modern jewellery. This kind of commercially imposed vandalism is more common today than it has ever been and, unlike the destruction of our architectural heritage, brought about by similar pressures, takes place privately and unchallenged.

It is not difficult to see why a diadem of base metal and yellow quartz should have escaped this ignominious end and appear at the *Antiques Roadshow* in Brighton. Despite its minimal intrinsic value, its maker had imbued it with all the grace and charm of grander jewels, and in choosing relatively humble materials had unwittingly ensured its preservation.

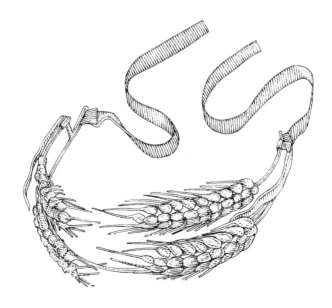

TALLBOY

John Bly

Giving popular names to English antique furniture has long been a useful means of describing in romantic and attractive terms what might otherwise sound plain and uninteresting. Lazy Daisy, for example, sounds so much more appealing than a revolving tray on stand. Canterbury is a nice name for what was originally just a plate stand. But surely the best of all is the tallboy.

This describes a chest of drawers made to stand on another chest of drawers or on an open base. Such two-part pieces of furniture have always been prone to separation and subsequent rematching, and this potential uncertainty gives such pieces added interest.

The earliest English tallboys date from the latter part of the seventeenth century and have a rather quaint appearance, slightly top-heavy on bases formed of delicate legs, which reminds me of a late seventeenth-century person in full costume. As the period progressed manufacture became more sophisticated and the turned legs were replaced by curved ones with a knee, an ankle and usually a pad foot. Gradually the space created by the open stand was filled with more drawers, until by the 1750s the tallboy became two chests of drawers, one standing on top of another.

There are many clues to help when dating tallboys. The drawers in early chests ran on side runners; these were fixed to the carcass or framework and a section called a rabbet was cut out of the sides of the drawers. By the 1720s the side runners had disappeared and the drawer ran on the bottom edges of its sides.

The decoration of the drawer fronts themselves helps. In the seventeenth century they were decorated around the edge with raised mouldings, giving the appearance of a recessed front, the centre of which bore the handle. In the early walnut period c.1690–1710 the drawer front was flush but had a moulding applied to the surrounding framework of the chest. By 1720 this had been superseded by a drawer front with edges which extended over the carcass, thus disguising the actual division between drawer and framework. Then, for the rest of the eighteenth century, 'cock beading' was added: a thin moulding, approximately 1/8 inch thick, was applied in a long strip to the edges of the drawer, standing proud of both drawer and frame.

Auction sales in the eighteenth century were rarely, if ever, attended by people of higher social standing than the vendor. So it is that we can still find things made for castles turning up in cottages. On the *Antiques Roadshow* in Hornchurch, Essex, I saw a tallboy which had actually been sawn in half, presumably because at some time in its history it wouldn't fit into its new home. With early furniture such drastic action surprisingly has no serious effect on its value if the two original halves have been reunited. But on later and more important pieces, where the damage is aesthetic as well as structural, such mutilation is a tragedy.

DAMAGE AND RESTORATION

David Battie

I WOULD GUESS THAT under 5 per cent of all the objects brought into *Antiques Roadshow* could be considered in perfect condition. Everything, including us, is in a process of natural decay, eventually to return to the elements from which it was made, and no amount of careful handling and protection can prevent this. All we can do is to delay it for as long as possible.

Some materials are more prone to rapid disintegration than others, textiles being an obvious example. Excepting gold, all metal objects, however hard, are changing from the minute they are forged or cast, to end as rust or oxides of copper or other components. Curiously, the more obviously fragile man-made materials such as glass and porcelain are in fact amongst the most resistant. Our earliest surviving man-made objects are the pots formed in prehistoric times.

Collectors will react to damaged objects in different ways, but must always take into account the age of the piece against the likelihood of another example having survived in good or better condition. If they decide to buy it, by how much should the price be reduced to take the damage into account? Collectors, certainly in today's market, seem to be less fastidious than in the past. This is the inevitable result of vastly increased collecting. There are simply fewer and fewer good examples to go round.

Why were so many thoroughly dreary broken pots stitched together in the past with rivets? The work was done largely by gypsies travelling the country undertaking odd jobs, and one suspects that many sherds were saved simply to give the gypsies something to do. Whatever the reason, we have to be thankful that many collectable pieces were saved which might otherwise have been thrown away. Today's skilled restorer can remove all trace of the holes.

So, should you have valuable objects restored? It all depends on why you have asked the question. If you intend keeping the object and the damage does not offend you or is invisible in the place where the object sits, why spend money on it? If it does offend – a missing hand from a figure is an obvious example – then restoration should be considered. If you are thinking of selling the piece, you should never restore it first. The buyer, whether a dealer, another collector or auction bidder, would rather see the piece with all its defects and make up his own mind.

Damage as such will never improve a piece, but two thousand years of burial have given Chinese Shang bronzes a patina upon which much of their price depends. The Japanese devotees of the Tea Ceremony who collect teabowls take the gold lacquer repairs to damaged pieces as part of the history, and the value is unaffected. If there's none so odd as folk, there's none odder than collectors: a maternally inclined friend of mine collects *only* damaged pieces because she feels sorry for them!

A COTTAGE
INDUSTRY

John Sandon

I T IS EASY TO FORGET that most of the objects we look at on the *Antiques Roadshow* were made for a specific purpose and would have been used by their original owners. Chairs were sat upon, dolls played with and teapots used for making tea.

Nineteenth-century models of rustic cottages may seem purely ornamental, but in the 1840s they played an important role in every house in the growing towns and cities. By modern standards the sanitation system in the centre of London was primitive beyond belief; typhoid and cholera were commonplace, and open sewers emptied directly into the Thames. Even in the smartest parts of the city the stench from the drains and from the river were frequently unbearable.

Sweet-smelling pastilles, burning very slowly, were used to fill the room with a scent which drowned the more unpleasant smells. The porcelain utensils in which the pastilles were placed were originally conical, but by the early Victorian period they had developed into a great variety of forms to remind their owners of the more fragrant countryside. Quaint ceramic cottages copied the follies which gentlemen built on their country estates to appear more rustic and tumbledown than the real thing. The finest were made of porcelain and are in two sections, the cottage lifting off its base in order to insert the pastille. Simpler types have an opening cut into the back to allow the conical pastille to be inserted. The base is pierced to allow air to circulate, the scented smoke drifting through the open chimneys, while in darkness the light given off by the burning pastille would glow very faintly through the pierced windows.

The majority of pastille burners were produced by small manufacturers in the potteries around Stoke on Trent. It is commonly believed that many were made at the Rockingham works, but while Rockingham did specialise in rustic porcelain, they never produced any houses or cottages. The whole attribution of these wares to the celebrated Yorkshire factory is totally unfounded.

The most valuable cottages today are those made by the leading Worcester factories as well as Coalport and Spode, with nice examples selling for well over £1000. Simple Staffordshire cottages can be collected from as little as £80, with typical examples costing between £200 and £300. A pale lilac or lavender ground instead of white will usually add considerably to the value, while any damage will naturally detract.

Ironically, it was a potter who brought about the downfall of the Staffordshire cottage. Henry Doulton made drainpipes and sanitary fittings which improved the air in every town, rendering the pastille burner obsolete. Some cottages remained popular as ornaments, and many later examples will be found without a hole cut into the back or with solid chimneys and windows. A great many were still being made from the original mould well into this century, and, sadly, modern fakes and reproductions are commonplace today. The same care has to be taken when buying a Staffordshire cottage as a real house in the country.

A SITTER FOR SCHWITTERS

Philip Hook

'THAT'S ME, PAINTED IN 1941.'

The portrait the lady was showing me at the Paignton *Antiques Roadshow* was of a little girl in a mood of contemplation. Besides being a sympathetic and sensitive study of a child, it was striking because it was painted in a powerful Expressionist style more German than English – an unexpected item to find on the Devon coast. Sure enough, it was signed with the initials KS, identifiable as those of the German artist Kurt Schwitters.

Schwitters occupies a significant place in the avant-garde of European twentieth-century painting. Born in 1887, he studied in Dresden and began to experiment with abstract painting in 1918. Soon he was a convert to Dadaism, a movement which needs some explanation. The Dadaists practised the creation of art out of objects not in themselves artistic. Thus the collage was invented – pictures made by sticking paper and other random items on to the canvas. Schwitters took this further, creating huge assemblages of objects, constructions which sometimes reached gigantic proportions and in one case almost filled an entire house. His raw materials were unusual – bits of lino, bus tickets, worn out shoe soles – the sort of arbitrary concoction dear to the Dadaists' hearts.

His unconventionality proved unacceptable to the Nazi regime, ever watchful for 'degeneracy' in art. So in 1937 Schwitters emigrated to Norway, but his stay there was short because the Germans invaded in 1940 and he had to move on again. He arrived in Britain as a refugee, and so it came about that he was put in touch with the family of the little girl in the portrait. They had volunteered to put up refugees in their house in the Lake District. She remembers his arrival, accompanied by a policeman to vouch for him.

He was a slightly eccentric figure, preferring to live off berries and goat's milk rather than more conventional food. But he grew deeply attached to the daughter of the house. 'He was like a grandfather to me,' she reminisced. 'I well remember him painting this portrait. My mother read me Beatrix Potter to keep me still.'

It was a rare *Roadshow* find, a fascinating human insight into one of the century's most innovative artists. The portrait itself may not have been an example of his most progressive work, but it sheds revealing light on Schwitters in informal mood. And by offering him shelter, the little girl's family were indirectly instrumental in creating a deeper understanding of Dadaism in this country. Schwitters stayed on and influenced a number of artists here before his death in 1948: one of his huge Dadaist constructions which he left unfinished at Ambleside was moved to Newcastle University in 1965, and collages by him are in the Tate Gallery in London.

CHINA: THE BRILLIANT MING

Lars Tharp

HONGWU, FOUNDER OF THE DYNASTY, gave it the name 'Ming'. The Ming Dynasty (1368–1644) was to be a brilliant one. So it was hoped and so it proved to be, politically and artistically. The name that had been chosen at its inception meant 'brilliant' itself. Let me explain.

The written Chinese language is pictographic: words (characters) are in many cases simplified pictures or depictions of the entity or thing actually represented. Thus 'brilliance' is conveyed by bringing together the characters for sun (small square) and moon (elongated crescent), combining into one character the heavens' brightest sources or reflections of light. This is the character for Ming.

By the early Ming Dynasty, porcelain was already a technically perfected art form. It was decorated with painting in underglaze blue and red (the latter with some difficulty); overglaze painting in a wide palette of clear enamels; combinations of under and overglaze painting; designs incised or carved into the porcelain itself, sometimes combined with colour or sometimes deliberately hidden in order only to be revealed when held against the light. And all of this was executed on a fine white porcelain potted into simple or complex forms, thick or near-eggshell thin. For a further four hundred years a number of European principalities strove to manufacture this magical material, not fully succeeding until 1710 with the first productions at Meissen in Saxony.

Meanwhile the dragon – that animal most associated with China – took up permanent residence on the bowls, dishes and vases made at the imperial command of the Dragon Throne itself. In the West we associate dragons with evil; in the East it is a creature of good omen with a creative, not destructive, power.

It represents the male principle of fertility. As such it is associated with water and its apparent effect of germination and generation: rain upon the rice-sown fields, the teeming plenty of the ocean. Wherever it appears the dragon inhabits clouds, rises from the waves, or twists between the mists and spume of both.

And so it appeared with unintended aptness on the late Ming blue and white bowl with which my client had for many years been watering her dog. When it was sold in 1983 and the story released to the press, one headline read: 'LAP OF LUXURY'. Being late Ming (from the Wanli Emperor period, 1573–1620) the bowl only fetched £5000.

Decorative motifs in Chinese arts can rarely be taken at face value. They may often contain deliberate visual puns due to the many homophones (words of identical sounds but of different meanings) in the language: thus five bats upon a vase automatically carry a wish to the receiver of 'a myriad happinesses' because that is what 'wu fu' (five bats) may also mean. A friend studying Chinese at university was one day delighted to discover in a classical text that 'the valley echoed with the mings of a thousand dragons'. In other words 'ming' is what dragons utter, as cats 'miaow'. Not very frightening in any language. Bearing in mind the Chinese fondness for picture puns, could

the reason for the popularity of the dragon in Ming times lie in the utterance of the dragon itself? 'Mi . . . ing'!? (I should mention for posterity that my friend's name is actually Robin Brilliant – or should it be Ming?)

JAPANESE CLOISONNÉ

David Battie

IN THE EARLY 1970s I was a cataloguer in a London saleroom, specialising in the nineteenth and twentieth centuries. Because there was no one else to do it I began to catalogue oriental works of art and was amazed by the beautiful and technically brilliant Japanese cloisonné. So excited was I by it, I even persuaded a client who asked me what I thought was undervalued at the time to buy a number of pieces.

Cloisonné is one of the few techniques to have made its way from the West to the Far East. Enamel (ground glass) is fused on to the metal shape within cells (cloisons) formed by wires fixed to the base. It was known in China from 1000 BC and made its way from there to Japan about AD 600, although little was produced until America severed Japan's isolation in 1853. From then on it was a story of ever-improving technique and increasing volume. By the turn of the century the whole town of Nagoya was dedicated to cloisonné, but Tokyo and Kyoto were also major centres.

The Japanese ability to crowd small areas with meticulous detail is well displayed on cloisonné, and their love of nature, real or imaginary, is brilliantly depicted. Small birds, their feathers picked out in silver and gold, flit from bamboo to prunus against a midnight sky. Dragons and phoenixes weave on a ground of gold-flecked aventurine above complex borders of scrolls and feathering. Unlike the bronzes and ivories of the Tokyo School, the human figure hardly ever appears.

The best pieces by masters such as Namikawa Sosuke, Namikawa Yasuyuki (no relation), Hayashi Kodenji and Ando Jubei make Fabergé's work look ham-fisted and can fetch up to £10 000 or more if signed. The signatures are all-important, as the market is dominated by American collectors who are particularly swayed by documentation. However, some unmarked pieces can be firmly attributed by comparison to signed pieces and surviving design books.

There are really two markets for cloisonné. One is a decorators' market where size is essential – the larger the better – and where 'in' colours such as green and yellow are more desirable than black or dark blue. On such pieces damage – normally a problem with cloisonné as it is almost unrestorable – is more acceptable. As with porcelain, a pair of vases is worth three times a single, although odd vases can be turned into desirable lamp bases.

Collectors are more interested in the small, finely crafted pieces. On the best examples the usual copper or brass wires are silver or occasionally gold. Another technique involves removing the cloisons with acid so that the colours flow like a watercolour painting. Whatever technique is used, the enamels are fired in a kiln and come out looking like an unretrievable blob. Then comes the time-consuming process of polishing which, on some of the better pieces, is known to have taken over a year.

Japan was a popular port of call on world cruises in the early 1900s and European and American tourists went on buying trips to visit typical Japanese craftsmen – usually an ivory carver, a potter, a weaver and a cloisonné maker. There is, therefore, a reasonable quantity available and on the *Roadshow* we have astonished many owners of cloisonné with the value of their pieces, which have risen dramatically over the last ten years. That original client of mine bought many of his pieces for under £100. They are now worth many thousands.

THE FAMILY BIBLE

Clive Farahar

O NE OF THE MOST ENDURING, consistent certainties of any *Antiques Roadshow* is that there will be at least one Bible in the book queue. People – who may be Christians, Muslims, Hindus or Seventh Day Adventists – have the belief that the very sanctity and antiquity of old Bibles lends them value. Some years ago, at a *Roadshow* in Watford, I counted nineteen large heavy family-type Bibles, and most of those were brought in by members of the Indian community.

The Bibles and Prayer Books that I see fall into two camps. On one hand there are the pretty little ones bound in soft leather, occasionally with ivory upper covers and perhaps a brass ornamental clasp or two. These for the most part were part of a lady's dress accessories for church, but quite useless for following the service: in a dimly lit church the small print would have been nearly impossible to read. The origin of these little pocket devotionaries goes back to the cradle of printing and beyond, into the garlanded field of illuminated manuscripts. However, the ones that I see tend to be those printed within the last 140 years. Their value relies on their elaborate decoration and the richness with which they were bound. The editions themselves are neither rare nor valuable.

In the other camp are the large Victorian family Bibles. These enormous thick quarto books, with a printed up space at the front to enter family members' names and dates, with plates occasionally in lurid chromolithography, maps and a central column concordance (references and explanatory notes), were designed for home consumption. In households where only the Bible was allowed to be read on Sundays, what a joy and relief these must have been. The pictures kept the youngest child happy, the maps and easy-to-read print were interesting to the older ones, and for the parent there was the family history to be entered in copperplate. For me, these Bibles mirror Victorian materialism and new money. The thick, leather-bound, sculpted covers, elaborately tooled with gilt arabesques, occasionally edged in brass-coloured metal securing two enormous clasps lying centrally on a chenille-covered parlour table, would have offered perfect evidence of the rectitude of the household.

Their present-day value rests on their condition. Sadly, with such heavy boards and the difficulty people have in storing them, finding one in near-mint condition is quite an event. Only once on the *Road-*

show has this happened to me. From a vacant child's pushchair, wrapped in a woolly shawl, appeared an almost perfect Victorian Bible. The leather was inky black and unscuffed, the gilt metal borders and clasps were unscratched, and the gilt tooling glowed in the television lights. They had bought it a few years before in a junk shop on the south coast for £5. I could not fault its condition – it was like new. Such a Bible must be worth £150 in a good second-hand bookshop, a real paragon of virtue.

WHAT PRICE YOUR TEDDY BEAR?

Bunny Campione

IN 1982 A CLIENT TOLD ME that she had a collection of teddy bears and asked if I would consider putting them up for auction. This was the time of Aloysius, Sebastian Flyte's teddy bear in *Brideshead Revisited*, and his owner Peter Bull – a wonderful man, sadly now dead – who was travelling throughout America with his teddies having teddy bears' picnics. America was already teddy crazy. 'So why not have a try. Let's see whether the market will take it,' I thought.

Approximately twenty-five teddy bears arrived at my office to be catalogued and put up for auction. Looking back, I realise that not one of them was by the famous German manufacturer Steiff. Amongst them was a black teddy bear with large ears and rather a pointed snout; his stuffing had shifted, causing his limbs and belly to flop around, which gave him a forlorn look. He was probably a 1910 English bear, and although not by Steiff he realised £360, which was the top price of the day. By 1985 teddies had started making big money. A Steiff teddy sold for £2000 in May of that year, making a new record and causing so much publicity that bears started coming on the market in profusion. Lots of much-loved and consequently worn examples started to troop into the *Antiques Roadshow*. But buyers became more discerning, preferring those teddy bears which had a trademark, were early and in good condition. Bears are not usually in excellent condition, so prices soared at the top of the market. In May 1988 a rare 1913 silver plush Steiff teddy bear in fine condition and with a muzzle realised £8800. I thought that would be it for a long time. Not so!

The new world record of £55 000 for the 1920 Steiff dual plush or 'bicolor' (so named by the Steiff factory) teddy is something of a fluke price and not one which should be relied upon as a yardstick for prices to come. A unique situation occurred: two buyers bid through agents, giving them no price limit. One has to sympathise with the new owner who had to pay so heavily. He was reportedly 'gobsmacked' when told what he had spent! The seller's immediate reaction was to say: 'That makes each hair worth £1000!' The lesson is that, however badly we want something, we should always place a price limit in advance.

For those hoping to retire on the back of their old teddies, how can you recognise the antecedents of your bear? German bears have extra-long arms and more pointed snouts. Steiff bears often have a trademark – a metal disc in the left ear which is difficult to remove. The earliest disc is embossed with an elephant for 1903–4, then a blank disc for 1904–5, and subsequently embossed with the name Steiff, with the tail of the last F finishing under the word. Age, condition, size and colour are all factors affecting value. Unfortunately the British-made bears such as Chad Valley, Chiltern, Dean's Rag Book Co., Ealon Toys, J. D. Farnell, Merrythought, Pedigree and Norah Wellings, to name but a few, while well made and just as appealing, do not yet command the same giddy price heights. Maybe they will one day!

THE REIGN OF THE MUSICAL BOX

Hilary Kay

T HERE IS NO SOUND which better soothes the queue at the *Antiques Roadshow* than the tinkling melody of a musical box. Fortunately several people at each *Roadshow* will struggle in with one of these bulky and heavy devices, pulling them along on shopping baskets behind them, or bringing them in the bottom of cavernous canvas carrier bags where they are discovered lurking like small coffins.

Surprisingly, the first musical boxes which created a melody by plucking a series of tuned steel teeth did not appear until the end of the eighteenth century, when a Swiss watchmaker began to incorporate simple musical movements into small objects such as watches, seals and vinaigrettes. It wasn't until the 1820s that musical boxes were produced as instruments in their own right. They came in small burr walnut boxes or larger ones made of ash, mahogany or rosewood containing the brass barrels, intricately pinned, which plucked the teeth as the barrel turned.

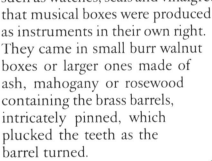

The majority of the musical boxes which I see at the *Antiques Roadshows* are those made in Switzerland in the 1870s, when mass production techniques, the tunes played and an export drive to Britain encouraged many households to buy. At a time when there was no recorded musical entertainment available it must have been an irresistible novelty to have music at the wind of the spring motor and the flick of the operating switch.

The Swiss makers were quick to exploit the market and soon produced musical boxes containing other instruments such as bells, snare drums and small organs, which encouraged the public to buy the latest model. Boxes were made with cylinders which could be interchanged so that a much larger repertoire of music was available than the eight, ten or twelve tunes which the majority of boxes were able to produce.

But it was with the disc musical boxes that real musical choice was offered to the public for the first time. Invented in Germany in the 1880s, disc musical boxes were produced in various sizes, from those with small 7-inch diameter discs capable of playing a limited number of notes on a small tuned steel comb to the 24-inch monsters which played complex melodies over several octaves. Extra metal discs could be bought on demand and popular music hall songs were quickly available in the shops. The smaller disc musical boxes (with up to about 15-inch diameter discs) were very attractive to ordinary households, and the cases could be quite ornate with Rococo styling or the use of decorative woods. The larger boxes were often coin-operated and were to be found in public places to provide musical entertainment, like contemporary juke boxes.

The reign of the musical box seemed unshakeable at the beginning of the century, but a revolution was to sweep away this musical monarch. In 1877 Thomas Edison had invented a way to record the human voice and in the early years of this century the phonograph and the gramophone deposed the musical box, sending it into obscurity, whilst laying the foundations for our generation of the radio, cassette tape and compact disc.

BRITISH AND GUARANTEED

Duncan Chilcott

I NEVER CEASE TO BE amazed at the number of train sets brought for inspection and valuation on the *Antiques Roadshow*. Famous makes such as Bassett-Lowke, Märklin, Bowman, Bing, Leeds Model Company and Lionel often turn up, but the most plentiful and popular are always the Hornby trains.

In 1901 Frank Hornby, who was employed by a Liverpool shipping company, patented a new toy, 'Mechanics Made Easy', soon to become known the world over as Meccano. It made his fortune. Later he introduced the ubiquitous Dinky toy for the enjoyment of generations of children and grown-up collectors alike.

But ever since 1920 the name of Hornby has been synonymous with toy railway trains produced at his world-famous Binns Road factory in Liverpool. He would be described as one of Mrs Thatcher's entrepreneurs if he were starting out today. During the First World War the firm made munitions, and despite the harsh Treaty of Versailles at the end of it the anti-German feeling in Britain was great enough to make even toys from Germany loathsome. This gave British goods the competitive edge, so Mr Hornby set out to diversify into model clockwork trains. By mid-1920 *Meccano Magazine* was able to predict the Hornby train: 'The builders are hard at work erecting great

new factories for us ... providing British boys and girls with British-made toys. ... Before next winter I shall be able to announce that we have ready for delivery the finest series of clockwork Railway Trains ever made.'

I still possess the Hornby train set given to me in 1964 when I was six years old. It is a plastic 'Ready to Run' Hornby Dublo Tank Goods Set No. 2001 with yellow open trucks, a red guards van, a quantity of track and blue power control unit. It cost £4 5s. (£4-25) when new in the sixties, and in good condition with its original box it's worth about £30 today.

The market favours the earlier 'O' gauge trains, one of which my father had as a boy. He was given it second-hand during the Second World War, when the Meccano/Hornby factory had to devote most of its manufacturing resources to government war contracts. According to the *Liverpool Evening Express* in December 1944, these ranged from 'bomb release units to fuses, from tools for fitting de-icing equipment to aircraft, to hypodermic needles'. In fact the production of Meccano and Hornby trains was prohibited under government order from the beginning of 1942.

My father's set was an 'O' gauge tinplate clockwork No. 2 4-4-0 'special'-type locomotive and six wheel tender in LMS red livery dating from around 1937–8, when it would have cost about £3. Today it would realise nearly £300 if in good condition with its original box! The No. 2 locomotives were the most popular and today the rarer ones like the *County of Bedford* locomotive and tender can make £500–600. The most exclusive 'Eton' locomotive has fetched £1000. My father also had a couple of green 1st/3rd class corridor passenger coaches, manual points and a large quantity of track, and he remembers that the locomotive was prone to derailing itself!

Sadly the Binns Road factory closed in 1980, further adding to the problems of the city of Liverpool, and though the Hornby name lives on today it will probably be for the products from Binns Road that the name will be best remembered: Hornby trains 'British and Guaranteed'.

Buyer Be Aware

Simon Bull

PEOPLE INTERESTED IN THE *Roadshow* often ask the question: 'What is the greatest rarity you have ever discovered on a show?' The short answer is that, although we find many unusual and sometimes valuable objects, the real rarities are very scarce.

Before the show in Birmingham I was sure I was on to something special when I was informed that a longcase clock by Edward East of London had been brought to the hall. East was one of England's premier clockmakers in the seventeenth century, and his work now fetches tens of thousands of pounds. Alas, it was not to be; although signed East, the signature was a fake, and the clock was only worth £4000 as a pleasant example of a marquetry case.

However, it reminded me of an occasion some twelve years ago when I was asked to visit a country house and value a clock by Ahasuerus Fromanteel, who was a contemporary of East's and an equally important maker. This clock was also something of a disappointment as, though genuine, it had been altered and was incomplete. The owner, a charming middle-aged lady, was most understanding and accepted my valuation of £4000, although she had obviously hoped for more (even then, such a clock in perfect state would have fetched over £8000). Her leaking roof forced her hand, and it was decided that I should remove the clock to London for sale.

My departure was delayed when the lady insisted that she had a winding key tucked away that would surely fit the clock. Keys, unless original, make no difference to the value, and I assured her it was unnecessary to launch a major search. No, she was certain it was around, and it would be nice for the new owner to have, and with that she crammed herself halfway into a small silver safe (a sort of un-windowed pantry with barred door that was often installed in old houses). I was left hopping from foot to foot, watching the fog descend gently like a blanket over the lawn, and listening to the sound of falling boxes of silverware accompanied by frequent, muffled progress reports. Eventually she reversed out of the safe, clutching the upturned lid of a shoe-box which contained all the goodies of an understair Aladdin's cave – broken bakelite plugs, fuse wire, labelled keys to long-forgotten dungeons, a clock key and – suddenly manners failed me. My arm shot out and I grabbed a dirty brass ball about the size of a small door knob which I had spied in the box. A quick twist and pull, and the ball split apart before the startled gaze of my host.

Inside was a pendulum-controlled watch movement suspended in a gimbal ring to keep it horizontal no matter the position of the ball (now that's an idea for railway coffee cups). Should I arrange for the sale of this too? 'Yes, of course,' she said. 'But do remember to take the key.'

After gentle cleaning the ball turned out to be beautifully engraved and gilded, with inscriptions around the outside and eight different portrayals of Cupid along with the owner's new monogram – probably a marriage gift. The movement was signed 'Madelainy A Paris'. It was only the second example to be discovered in a complete state, the other already being in a museum. That was twelve years ago, and it was sold for over £20 000.

Oh . . . and the Fromanteel fetched a respectable £4500.

DIRT IN THE ENGRAVING

Ian Harris

W HEN I FIRST STARTED working in the silver trade thirty-five years ago we handled quite a lot of different things that we seldom handle now: cut-glass lustres, china dessert services, ormolu; we even used to make rather good Louis pattern tea sets (the ones with a funny-looking face at the base of the spout, and an eagle as the finial*) as well as dealing in antique silver and plate. One of the things I used to see quite a lot was niello work. It's a fairly minor decorative art, but an attractive one.

Silver is a pleasing metal, for which niello provides an effective foil. Made of a mixture of silver sulphide, copper and lead, it is a shiny dark grey when polished and goes rather pewtery in appearance when not. It melts at a fairly low temperature. The piece of silver to be decorated is engraved, and the powdered niello applied into the engraving. The piece is then heated to around 1200°C, melting the powder. Any surplus is polished away, and what remains contrasts most effectively with the silver background.

Some of the best-known experts at niello were the Russians; many of their pieces are very finely engraved, and the finest ones partially or completely gilded. When I was in Dallas recently I bought a lovely sweet basket luxuriating in over-blown roses, probably from southern Russia or Turkey. The technique is also widely used around the Mediterranean, especially in Egypt, and as far east as Thailand.

Niello was used from very early times, although the majority of the pieces that have survived date from the eighteenth and nineteenth centuries. The subjects in the eighteenth century were almost invariably figurative and in the nineteenth century

---

* Finial – a decorative knob applied to furniture or on the covers of vessels made in silver, pottery, porcelain and glass.

architectural, especially on the many snuff boxes showing popular scenes of Moscow and St Petersburg. Another eighteenth-century type had maps of campaigns and explorations.

The French too were fond of niello boxes in the nineteenth century, but their designs tended to be of all-over floral or geometric patterns. They really don't have the charm and character of the Russian ones, which is probably why they don't cost as much – say £600–700, whereas the Russian variety can make £1000–1500.

Buckles in niello work turn up quite consistently. Similar ones were also made in cloisonné enamel. They are generally Russian and bear the St Petersburg mark. The Russian hallmarking system is one of the most comprehensive and marks are mostly listed in a work known as 'Goldberg' – so-named after one of its joint authors; the other's name is unpronounceable!

As I said, we used to stock quite a lot of it, but not for some time. So I suppose it was to be expected when one of my cleaners came up to me with a recently acquired snuff box and said, 'I've been working on this for four days and I can't get the dirt out of the engraving'!

AN ELEPHANT WITH ALMOND-SHAPED EYES

Victoria Leatham

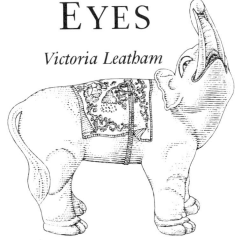

E VER SINCE THE JAPANESE began trading with the West during the seventeenth century (although they still denied access to their territory to foreigners until 1853), they have displayed a knack of supplying what the market requires. Today, videos and cameras; then, ceramics. Due to internal warfare in China the great porcelain-producing nation was unable to export to the West. The Japanese seized their chance and the market gratefully absorbed whatever they delivered. It was mostly in the Chinese idiom and traditionally decorated in underglaze blue.

In 1661 everything changed. For the first time Japanese *over*glaze enamels appeared in Europe. Imagine the excitement as the weary little trading vessels opened their holds to disclose their startling multi-coloured cargoes. The merchants had never encountered anything like it before. Quite what galvanised the potters and painters in Arita to start enamelling is not clear, but their chosen palette of red, blue, turquoise, black and yellow was copied for the next two hundred years by factories such as Bow, Chelsea, Meissen and Chantilly.

Amongst the range of these objects made in the seventeenth century, the enchanting animals are my favourites. The energy and enthusiasm of the modeller is not always matched by accuracy, however. I have seen a pair of fine elephants incongruously modelled with almond-shaped oriental eyes. The man who created them had never seen an elephant. After all, his own eyes were that shape, so why not the elephant's? There were hundreds of different animals and birds made and, although it would be unfair to describe them as naive, they have the same simple vitality as early Staffordshire wares.

We know so little about the distribution of porcelain from quayside to client. How did people buy? Did they go to shops or order from dealers, who were known as china men? How is it that a wealthy Duke in Nottingham could have the same pieces as another Duke in Bedfordshire? We simply don't know. All we can say for certain is that there was a strong element of competition amongst Their Graces. These oriental treasures were very pricey, and it was a social triumph to have your mantelpiece groaning under the weight of coloured hawks, dogs, fish and a myriad other creatures, newly arrived from Japan. They were considered far superior to the outmoded *blanc-de-chine* and blue and white of former times. As well as figures the Japanese supplied plates, bowls, dishes and anything else that was ordered, sometimes decorated in rich floral designs in red, blue and gold which we now recognise as 'Imari'.

Eventually the Chinese sorted out their troubles and re-entered the fray. The Japanese took second place in the export trade and this remained the case for about two hundred years, until in the 1950s an authority on Japanese ceramics, Soame Jenyns, published books extolling their virtues. The wheel has spun full circle, and nowadays the prices fetched by seventeenth-century Japanese pieces in salerooms are astonishing. Recently at auction a plate painted in overglaze enamels bearing the 'Hob-in-the-Well' pattern was sold for £27 000. In the main the buyers are Japanese, purchasing back their heritage. The Americans are next in line, with many keen collectors. The poor old British, who originally led the world in the appreciation and acquisition of these beautiful objects, are now either outbid as buyers or have turned to providing the goods for sale.

BORN WITH A SILVER SPOON

Ian Pickford

THE EXPRESSION 'born with a silver spoon' goes back to the period when a spoon was presented to a child at the time of baptism. The quality of the spoon would depend on the wealth of the family and the material from which it was made would range from wood or horn, pewter and brass, to silver and even gold.

In the seventeenth century and earlier you would have to be born of good yeoman or merchant stock or even higher to receive a silver spoon. That spoon would normally be the one you used for the rest of your life. At any banquet you attended you took your own spoon and knife with you: none would be provided. Forks did not appear until the end of the seventeenth century. Before then most food, if solid enough, was eaten with the hands.

Since the type of spoon produced at a banquet was a good indication of your wealth, spoons became a status symbol. As a result, the first piece of silver you would buy on working your way up through society would normally be a spoon. Some people cheated and had brass spoons silvered to make it look as though they were higher up the social scale! Later, if 'selling the family silver' was forced upon you, you would normally try to hold on to your spoon to the very last.

From this it is clear that many early spoons must survive – and are there to be collected. A thirteenth- or fourteenth-century example turned up not so long ago in a kitchen drawer, and a fantastic fourteenth-century spoon was found in a thatched roof! The former was sold for £1250, and the one from the roof made nearly £15 000.

During the Elizabethan period the length of spoons increased from about 6 to 7 inches. The earlier, shorter stem was fine to use with a good medieval shovel action, but the longer versions became necessary because of the change to the modern way of using spoons.

The tops or knops have all sorts of fascinating devices on them. The most famous are the Apostles, although my favourites must be the Wodewose (Wild Man of the Woods), now better known as the Green Man, and the 'Demi Female'. This voluptuous naked lady came from the West Country and was probably based on a ship's figurehead.

You have to be careful that the tops are original. On one *Roadshow* I was shown a provincial Apostle spoon that had been converted from a much more common form. It was worth only a fraction of what the owner had recently paid for it. Some genuine sixtenth- and seventeenth-century examples have appeared and there must be many more out there. So often I hear, 'I've got an old spoon at home but I didn't bring it because I didn't think it would be of much interest.' Think again!

'HERE I AM'

David Battie

A RECENT TAXI RIDE along the Embankment in London past Cleopatra's Needle reminded me of one of the few examples of Egyptian antiquity which we have seen on the *Roadshow*. The ancient Egyptians seem to have spent a great deal of their waking life preparing themselves for life after death, and most of their surviving works of art have been found in tombs. The hot, dry climate could hardly be bettered as a preservative and, sealed in airless caves or deep in pyramids, objects are unaffected by their two thousand years of burial. Not only have works of art been preserved but so have their owners, their bodies mummified along with sacred ibises, cats and crocodiles.

Interred alongside the deceased were all possible comforts to see him on his journey to the afterlife: food, drink, furniture, regalia and, once the practice of burying servants with the dead had ended, models of servants to minister to him. The most common object to accompany the body would be the Shabti figure, a worker equipped with various tools who could perform any task that the resurrected master needed. Surprisingly, such everlasting devotion can be had for a relatively small sum – a poor example for £60, the bulk £400–800 and the very best a few thousand: this for a work of art two and a half thousand years old. The less well-modelled and glazed examples would have been made for the poorest classes, but the finest are exquisite pieces of miniature sculpture.

They are glazed in tones which range from a dull green to an almost fluorescent turquoise, for blue was the colour of eternal resurrection and renewal. Many have either incised or painted inscriptions in hieroglyphics from the Sixth Book of the Dead, which instruct the Shabti to perform his tasks for the deceased. When called on by his master, the Shabti was to reply: 'Here I am.'

The material used to fabricate them dates back to the fourth millennium BC and is peculiar to Egypt. It is a form of faience – a very soft, granular quartz or sand bonded by heat with alkali from plant ash to give a partly vitreous body. The glazes, often thick and bubbled, were also alkali with a low melting point and coloured with malachite or copper. The figure usually takes the form of a tightly bandaged, mummified body, its hands crossed over the chest. It stares out at the world with an expression of mild amusement as unfathomable as that of the Sphinx. Although only 7 inches high the figure has a monumental quality that seems to radiate a power and mystery quite out of proportion to its size.

Ceramics are amongst the first artifacts made by any developing society and, despite their apparent fragility, are great survivors. Long after I have vanished, probably long after mankind has disappeared from the face of the earth, there will still be Shabti figures waiting in the hot sands of Egypt for the final orders of their masters . . . and still wearing that smile.

ROMANS AT THE BOTTOM OF YOUR GARDEN

Henry Sandon

THE EXCITEMENT GENERATED by London's first view of the Portland Vase in 1784 turned many into avid collectors of antiquities. Sir William Hamilton's great collection of Greek and Roman vases in the British Museum and the publication of the catalogue in 1766-7 had already turned contemporary taste away from the frivolity of Rococo and Chinoiserie into imitations of the shapes and designs that were being unearthed from Etruscan tombs and the ruins of Herculaneum and Pompeii.

This new 'revival of the arts' as it was termed (later called Neo-classicism) led Josiah Wedgwood to pursue it avidly. He used 'jasperware', a type of hard unglazed pottery, in colours that seemed to mirror the Classical world, to make fifty or so copies of the Portland Vase, which were issued in 1790. Only sixteen of these originals are known to survive and any one of them could be said to be 'beyond rubies', as the good book says. An old lay clerk colleague of mine in Worcester Cathedral choir, after we had sung those words in an anthem, used to quip: 'What was Ruby's price?' So perhaps we might hazard a guess that the value could be £25 000 and upwards, although a good nineteenth-century copy might be obtained for £500 or so.

I would like to have been part of Sir William Hamilton's

entourage in Naples and to have gone with him to purchase Etruscan vases. The excitement of stepping back in time and finding something ancient in the ground is a wonderful feeling. To realise that you are the first person to see the object for hundreds or thousands of years is humbling and can change the course of a person's life, as it did with me.

I first went to Worcester as a professional musician, and it was while living in a medieval house in the shadow of the Cathedral that I carried out an excavation in my garden. It was fascinating peeling away the layers of history, working back through the centuries until I reached the Roman levels at a depth of 10 feet. There was my first Roman.

I don't know if you've ever been face to face with a dead Roman in your garden. If you have, you will know that it is quite a shock. I believed that you had to report the finding of a body, so my wife cleaned up the skull, which I then put in a box and took to the police station. At the counter was a huge policewoman who boomed at me in a fine bass voice, 'What do you want?'

'I've come to report finding a body.'

'What sort of body?'

'A human body,' I said. 'I've got his head in the box.'

She called for the sergeant and I was steadily passed up the ranks, rather like 'Sam, pick up tha musket', until we got to the Chief Inspector, who seemed to harbour suspicions that I had done it.

An inquest was held on the poor fellow in my garden, and I was able to prove that I was innocent because of the Roman pottery found with him. I was let off with a caution and a growing respect for Roman pottery, especially for a large second-century AD storage jar which had been mended with metal rivets in Roman days. The obvious affection that the Roman had for his pot transferred to me, turning me into a potaholic, unable to keep my hands off pots.

A STRANGE GENESIS

Lars Tharp

HAD THEY BEEN ITALIAN we might not have been so surprised. But the four Old Testament prophets which were brought to us by a Danish farmer on the *Antiques Roadshow* from Sweden had come from East Asia.

The gilt bronze figures were approximately 6 inches high and embellished overall in colourful enamels applied into cells gouged out of the cast metal or into a network of applied wires. These two techniques are respectively known as champlevé and cloisonné enamelling. Immediately recognisable was Moses, striking a pose similar to the statue of him by Michelangelo. However, the Tablets bearing the Ten Commandments were written not in Hebrew, Latin or any European language, but Chinese, translating as 'The Three Imperatives and the Seven Prohibitions'. How had Judeo-Christian figures executed in China, following apparently Italian Baroque models, surfaced in Scandinavia?

That the figures were intended for the Chinese market is clear from the Chinese inscription on Moses' Tablets. Although it is possible that the intended Chinese client was interested in the figures from a merely decorative point of view, it is also possible that he would have been in tune with the religious significance of the prophets. Chinese cloisonné figures of human form, of whatever period, are exceptionally rare, and though appropriate to both Jewish and Christian faiths it is tempting to speculate that the figures may have come into existence for or via the Jesuit mission in Peking.

When furnishing his Summer Palace in the European style in the 1750s, the Qianlong Emperor was guided by French and Italian missionaries who provided exotic European works of a Baroque style for the project. The work was co-ordinated by the Italian Jesuit Giuseppe Castiglione, himself a highly accomplished painter and the designer of the twelve life-size bronze animals which formed a time-keeping Great Fountain at the foot of the palace. Castiglione died in 1766, thirty years before the death of his Imperial patron.

The four small prophets which appeared in Sweden had all apparently come from a larger composition, in that each had an integral bar underneath centred by a threaded hole, obviously for attachment to a presumably common base. Might such a larger work have been suitably impressive and exotic for the Emperor's European palace, while promoting through art the Jesuits' ultimate missionary purpose?

After his death in 1797 the Qianlong's favourite palace fell into decay and was near dereliction when, in 1860, it was plundered by French and English troops. In this way a number of works 'liberated' from the palace came on to the European market. Among the booty offered for sale at the auction rooms of Drouot in Paris in December 1861 were '*très-beaux émaux cloisonné*' ('very fine cloisonné enamels'). The Danish owner of the four prophets told us that he had inherited the figures from his late wife, whose father had been given them by an Italian refugee in recognition for his services in assisting his flight from Mussolini's Italy to Switzerland.

Stylistically the figures are based on sixteenth-century European originals. Technically (judging from the colours and patterns used in the enamel work) they would have been made in the eighteenth or nineteenth century. Without further evidence it is not possible to support or deny a possible association of these figures with the Jesuit mission in Peking or as part of a composition perhaps intended for the Summer Palace. What is certain is that they are exceptionally rare, maybe unique. By way of the *Roadshow* coming to Scandinavia they have now come into the limelight for full discussion.

THE MASTER MODELLER

Hugo Morley-Fletcher

MANY PEOPLE THINK that unmarked pieces of porcelain are unlikely to be of interest. Yet because it is always the earliest pieces that have no mark, they are potentially the most fascinating.

The two small 1730s' Meissen figures by Kändler which I was shown at the Elsinore *Antiques Roadshow* were unmarked. Even when the Meissen crossed swords mark was used it was very small and placed on the back of the base, not underneath. Unless you know where to look, you are unlikely to spot it. The colouring was very simple with a few strong colours applied only to the figure, leaving the bases plain white. It may be this very simplicity and lack of identifying marks which accounts for the scarcity of pieces that are brought to us on the *Antiques Roadshow*.

A factory was set up at Meissen in 1710 after the secret of making porcelain was finally discovered in Germany. For the first twenty years the pieces produced were unlike the wares and figures we take for granted today. Then Johan Joachim Kändler appeared and changed everything. Between 1730 and 1740 he entirely revolutionised the use to which porcelain was put and the way in which it was moulded and decorated. Until he came along, plates, vases and tureens had been basically flat. Kändler moulded the entire surface with scrolls and relief patterns and shaped the rims of plates and dishes. Figures had hitherto been large, competing with sculpture. Kändler was the first to see that the ideal scale was small, generally 6–9 inches high, and that there was a vital relationship between the individual model and the way that it was coloured. His output was prodigious. He modelled a wide range of figures of Harlequin, the key figure of the popular Italian comedy, and he created a whole series of figures of animals and birds which were extraordinary for the lifelike effects he was able to obtain. His power of observation must have been quite exceptional. Kändler kept a journal which he called his 'Taxa' in which he kept a record of what he did. This, which is still at the factory, gives us a very clear picture of his activity as a porcelain modeller.

Because the Meissen factory was established almost twenty-five years earlier than any other manufacturers in Germany, Italy and England its influence, and therefore that of its *Modellmeister* Kändler, is to be seen everywhere. The younger factories sometimes just took a Meissen figure, made moulds from it and produced their own version. This practice was followed by Chelsea, Bow, Derby and Loughton Hall in England, at many of the minor German factories and at Doccia and Capodimonte in Italy.

The number of Meissen figures and groups made during Kändler's time at the factory was large, and many were imported into Britain. It is reasonable to expect to see them more often than we do. Why not have another look in your china cabinet and bring what you've got to an *Antiques Roadshow* recording?

A FINE EXAMPLE

Christopher Payne

THE ANTI-GALLACIAN SOCIETY may sound like a group of conservative scientists from an H. G. Wells novel. In fact the society was formed not to protect us from outer space but from France, or at least French trade and design. It was established in 1745 by the distinguished but little-known designer Thomas Johnson whose own work, perversely, was in the new Rococo style that had recently arrived from France. He interpreted Rococo plant and shell forms, mixing them with animals and birds, as well as scenes from Aesop's Fables. These plant-like forms lent themselves to the dexterity of the English carver's art and there were several other designers working with them, amongst them Thomas Chippendale.

Chippendale is possibly more famous today than he was amongst his contemporaries. His name lives on for his comprehensive book of designs, *The Gentleman and Cabinet-maker's Director*. First published in 1754, the *Director* proved so successful that it was published again with little alteration in the following year, and again in 1762, this time with fifty new plates. The publication itself was intended as a commercial exercise, 333 copies of the first edition selling for £1 10s. (£1.50) in loose-leaf form. His engraver Matthew Darly, who appears to have done most of the work, also published his own designs and those of the firm of Ince and Mayhew.

Chippendale's ploy worked. He sold his designs, at the same time attracting lucrative and important commissions for his finished work. The most notable of these was for Harewood House in his native Yorkshire, a house remarkably intact and open to the public today.

His influence travelled abroad to Germany and on into the next century when Victorian designers rediscovered Chippendale's work, often with somewhat quaint results. Chippendale became a household name now used popularly to describe that rich period at the end of George II's reign and the beginning of George III's, a period of carved and plain mahogany furniture which has now adorned many English houses for generations, building up a wonderfully rich patination over the last two hundred years. A fine pair of chairs that I saw on the Tunbridge Wells *Antiques Roadshow* were typical of this Chippendale style.

Chippendale was a canny man, born in the North of England in 1718 and becoming a respected London businessman in the third quarter of the century. He was a man who demanded a very high standard from his craftsmen, but was arguably more creative in business than in his originality of design. His thriving firm was aided by his willingness to take risks. In 1769 he imported from France sixty chair frames, which he declared as being worth a mere £18. The vigilant customs seized his goods, realising that Chippendale had declared the frames simply as lumber and had attempted to import them in pieces to lessen their apparent value.

I wonder how Thomas Johnson and the Anti-Gallacian Society would have regarded this dubious activity?

MARKS OF RECOGNITION

Terence Lockett

WALK INTO A RESTAURANT almost anywhere in the world and observe the customers. Before long you will see someone surreptitiously lift the plate in front of them, turn it over and inspect the back. You can be pretty confident that you have spotted a collector. It's the same on the *Antiques Roadshow*. Hand a plate to Henry Sandon, David Battie or one of the other porcelain experts, and no matter how marvellous is the decoration on the front, within two seconds the back of the piece is being eagerly scrutinised.

English potters rarely marked their wares with their own names until, almost inevitably, Josiah Wedgwood made a distinctive feature of having his name impressed in the clay before the ware was fired. The early porcelain factories such as Chelsea and Derby had used marks like anchors or crowns, but not the factory or potter's name. But by 1820 most wares carried if not the name of their maker, at least his initials or some identifiable mark. In addition, many pieces carried a factory pattern number on the back. Chinese potters had been marking their wares for centuries; and European manufacturers too, such as Meissen and Sèvres, had used marks of identification, though not normally the actual potter's name.

If you wish to identify the tea set left to you by your great-aunt, there are plenty of reference books containing huge lists

of marks – those compiled by Geoffrey Godden and John Cushion are available from most libraries. But some marks still defeat the experts. Who is 'W(***)'? Examination of wares so marked tell us he is probably a Staffordshire potter of the period 1790–1810. Though he was once thought to be Enoch Wood, recent research suggests that this is not the case. Ten pounds will gladly be awarded by the writer to any reader who can provide positive documentary proof of the identity of the mysterious potter who used the 'W asterisk' mark!

DAVENPORT

The mark illustrated above gives almost all you need to know about the piece. It is impressed 'Davenport' over an anchor, at either side of which are the numbers '3 6' which tell us that the piece was potted in 1836 by the Staffordshire firm of Davenport. The printed pattern name 'Waverley' indicates that it is one of a series of illustrations from the novels of Sir Walter Scott. The third mark is that of the American importer to whom this particular piece had been despatched. The picture on the front is rather boring after all that.

When next you see a person turn over a plate don't think them rude. They may be simply 'Chinamaniacs' – or, in more modern terms, 'psycho-ceramic'. And it could all be quite official. They are probably members of the 'Plate Turn Over Club', which entitles them to 'turn over any plate in any hotel or restaurant . . . without penalty etc. . . . . Valid World Wide'. The plastic cards are a neat sales gimmick by one of the oldest firms in the industry – who always marked their wares.

THE FAKER'S ART

Philip Hook

AT AN *Antiques Roadshow* in the town hall at Manchester, I was shown a painting which for a moment I thought was by Lowry. It was a typical townscape with the familiar matchstick figures, but close examination and a consultation with the local museum soon established beyond doubt that it was an out-and-out fake.

Fakes can be very difficult to detect with certainty. In 1989 an authority on French twentieth-century painting denounced as fakes several pictures by Utrillo which were about to be sold at a London auction. Another authority on the artist disagreed, claiming them to be genuine. The art world and the public watched in dismay. No one likes the thought of shelling out £100 000 for an apparently genuine Utrillo, only to be told that it is an imitation with a real value of perhaps £1000.

There are two sorts of fake at large in the market. Out-and-out fakes, such as the Utrillos were alleged to be, are deliberate forgeries painted by imitators copying the style of a great artist and occasionally taking the criminal step of adding a false signature. There is no legal restriction on painting a picture in another person's style; the criminal act is in appending a

'wrong' signature, or in misrepresenting the picture as genuine to a prospective buyer.

The second sort of fake is rather different. This is an older picture, from the nineteenth century or earlier, which started life as a perfectly honest 'school' picture, a work by a follower or pupil of the more important names. Over the years these pictures have come to be attributed to the masters themselves, as the identity of their original creators faded into obscurity. Sometimes, later on, other hands have added false signatures to help them on their way, but they remain what they are: straightforward, second-grade paintings lacking the quality to be the work of the masters concerned.

The modern faker is helped by the way that twentieth-century painting has developed. Originally, most painters aimed essentially to paint nature, to reproduce what they saw. In the last hundred years painting has taken a less representational and more self-expressive direction, and personal style has become the distinguishing mark. When you no longer have the standard of 'truth to nature' by which to judge the quality of a painting, you are more likely to be deceived. In addition, a modern forger who tries to paint a Rembrandt using present-day materials would soon be found out because it's impossible to reproduce convincingly the patina and the cracking of age. With a modern masterpiece – a Utrillo, for instance – he has much more chance of avoiding detection by technical analysis.

Herring, Morland, Constable, Turner, Rembrandt, Corot; these are perhaps the most faked older names. As the old joke goes, there are a thousand genuine Corots in the world, and two thousand of those are in America. In the case of these older masters, experience and expertise can tell the fake from the genuine fairly easily. But with the more modern productions, the Utrillos of this world, a decision is more difficult. In order to confirm their authenticity the expert needs to rely more heavily on outside evidence such as provenance – the established history of the picture and its previous ownership. Where this information doesn't exist, he must tread carefully. The next person to bring an undocumented Utrillo into the *Antiques Roadshow* will doubtless receive a polite but very guarded verdict.

DANGER – UNEXPLODED ANTIQUE!

Bill Harriman

THOSE OF US WHO are intrepid enough to deal with the arms and militaria section of the antiques scene have to be able to turn our hands to many skills, not the least being handling live munitions! During the course of my working life I have been considerably alarmed, nay terrified, by such potentially explosive artifacts as spill holders made from cartridge cases, door stops from artillery shells, letter openers of hammered shrapnel, and paperweights from various bits of ordnance. Whilst these are interesting and decorative, the very real possibility that they might still be live is never far from my thoughts.

So you will be able to picture my consternation when, during the Glenrothes *Antiques Roadshow*, a gentleman rummaged in his bag and deposited on my table what appeared to be a grenade! After the massive rush of adrenalin had subsided and my pulse rate had returned to normal, I gingerly examined the curious object in more detail. It looked like a large cast-iron baby's rattle. The body, which was the size of a tennis ball, was hollow and had a wooden handle. On the top was a collar over which was fitted a mushroom-shaped button which was retained by a split pin running in a groove. When this was removed, a small nipple for a percussion cap was revealed.

The owner thought that this might have been an anti-poaching device that was filled with gunpowder, primed with a percussion cap and hung upside down from a tripwire. When the hapless poacher snagged the wire, the device would fall to the ground, the cap would be struck by the button and the gunpowder exploded, showering the neighbourhood with pieces of cast-iron shrapnel. A plausible explanation, but I think unlikely as the considerable blast would have caught not only the rural miscreant but also the entire covert and pheasants it was designed to protect!

I think, though I have never seen one like it before or since, that it was really a form of self-activating grenade probably dating from the Crimean War (1854–6) or the American Civil War (1861–5). In both conflicts there was much trench warfare, in which grenades would have been very handy.

The earliest grenades were just cast-iron spheres filled with powder and ignited by a length of perilously spluttering fuse. Naturally, these could be as lethal to the thrower as to the recipient. Thus ways of making grenades explode only when they hit their targets were always being sought. In the case of the Glenrothes grenade, the plucky grenadier would have bowled the device overarm like a cricket ball, its weight causing it to strike the ground nose first, exploding the charge.

Grenades are becoming collectable, and the market for them is rising. Recently I saw a First World War stick grenade realise £85, and even the humble Mills No. 36 'pineapple' grenade now commands between £25 and £40. Three years ago you might have picked one up for a fiver. I have always found them fascinating and would recommend them to a collector looking for something out of the ordinary (there are over eighty British types alone).

I must temper my enthusiasm with a word of warning, however obvious: always ensure that your piece of military history is empty and unprimed. If you have any doubts, then leave it alone and contact the police immediately. Otherwise your day might go off with a real bang!

A WISE
INVESTMENT

Henry Sandon

THE LOCALLY MADE antique speciality rarely turns up at a *Roadshow*, perhaps because it has long since moved from its place of origin. How else can you explain finding three outstanding ceramic items from Worcester, Yorkshire and Staffordshire in Northampton, where everyone expected only boots and shoes to walk in?

Two of the items were a beautiful Royal Worcester porcelain dessert service painted with cattle and a boisterously cheerful Yorkshire dish, naively decorated with a bird. Then out of a lady's bag containing the obligatory bits of twentieth-century Japanese eggshell porcelain and German figurines that turn up at every *Roadshow* fluttered a slipware owl. Made in north Staffordshire in the late seventeenth century, these were used as amusing drinking cups, the strong liquor being poured from the body of the owl into the head, from which you drank. Its red clay body was covered in different coloured slips – the term for liquid clays – which were put on in sequences, perhaps white first on the original red body, then dark on the white for contrast. The method of application ranged

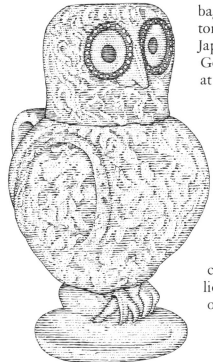

from dipping to – most elaborate of all – trailing from a slip trailer, like a pastrycook decorating a cake with icing. The slip could be left in thick globules, as were the brown dots around the owl's eyes, or treated in an imaginative way by 'feathering' two different coloured slips together, dragging one through the other with a point. The result looked rather like the decoration on a Bakewell tart.

Slipware is a very traditional English craft which flourished in the seventeenth century at Wrotham in Kent, where they made multi-handled drinking cups known as tygs. In Staffordshire one of the greatest exponents of the craft was Thomas Toft, who wielded his slip trailer like a master painter's brush, producing large dishes that are beautiful and moving. Although the discovery of harder-wearing and more practical ceramic bodies rang the death knell of slipware in the eighteenth century, some country potters kept the flag flying and there are a number of young craftsmen potters nowadays who have rediscovered the skills.

There in front of me in Northampton sat the owl, rare and wonderful. Although it was nearly three hundred years old and made in soft pottery, the only damage it had sustained was a slight crack in the neck and abrasions to the body – no doubt through use. It had been in the lady's family as far back as they could remember. She called him Ozzie Owl. Into my mind came the words of the poet Shelley: 'Rarely, rarely comest thou, spirit of delight.'

Editor's note: The owl was subsequently sold at auction for just over £20 000 and can now be seen at the Stoke on Trent City Museum.

COLLECTING SUGAR CRUSHERS

John Sandon

For those of us who cannot afford rarities like the Northampton slipware owl, the trick is to find something which is so far unappreciated by collectors. A few years ago my wife did exactly that.

'I've bought a swizzle stick,' she proudly told me, showing me a rod of twisted glass which had cost her 50p in our local junk market. I had to correct her, of course.

'It's actually a sugar crusher,' I replied, adding that they were very common and not worth anything.

She sensed a challenge. 'Right, in that case I'll collect them!' she declared, embarking on an obsession which five years later has resulted in a collection of three hundred examples.

Sugar crushers date from the time when you couldn't buy bags of granulated sugar. Instead you had to break lumps off a sugar loaf and place them into your hot drinks with sugar tongs. To help them dissolve it was necessary to grind the softening lump against the inside of the glass or cup – which is what these slender sticks were used for.

I have had great difficulty researching the history of sugar crushers, as virtually no records survive. I believe the earliest were made of clear glass in the middle of the eighteenth century. By the 1780s silver was used to make very fine-quality twisted examples, and several are known with hallmarks from the end of the eighteenth century. These are now very rare, although Sheffield Plate examples can occasionally be found for only a few pounds. Checking the lists of products of the early glass-producing houses I have found no mention of sugar crushers, even though their production must have been widespread. The only contemporary evidence I have found is a sketch by the caricaturist Thomas Rowlandson which shows a drunken meeting after a hunt. A reveller sits holding a drinking

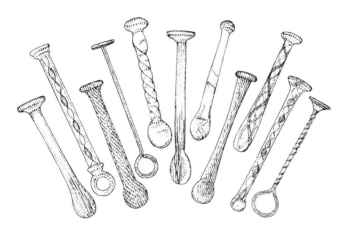

glass known as a 'rummer'. In his other hand he lifts up a small stick, which I take to be a sugar crusher, with which to offer a toast.

Most seem to date from the middle of the Victorian era. They range from clear rods with the simplest flattened end, to those with elaborate ends squeezed between patterned moulds. The most ornate are twisted like barley sugar and can be as long as 7 inches, although most are between 5 and 6 inches. Rarely recognised for what they are, clear glass examples can be bought remarkably cheaply. My wife has never paid more than £3 and most cost between 75p and £1.50.

The exceptions are the rarities made in coloured glass. Solid blue and green colours are associated with Bristol, and those encapsulating twisted glass are known by the term Nailsea, after the glass works near Bristol famed for making novelties. In reality 'Bristol' and 'Nailsea' glass was made all over the country. These would cost you between £30 and £60 each if you went to a specialist dealer, although most of my wife's were bought for far less because they were unrecognised.

Few other items in Victorian glass offer such variety and can still be found so easily for such little money. Long and thin twentieth-century examples made by machine, as well as modern glass cocktail sticks, add colour to my wife's decorative collection of antique sugar crushers. I am now fully converted and glad she didn't listen to me when I advised her against buying such valueless things.

HEADS OF STATE

Terence Lockett

O N THE *Antiques Roadshow* at Leominster I was shown a statuette depicting the seated figure of the Victorian statesman Lord Palmerston. At first glance it appeared to be made of marble. This is what was intended. In fact it is made of a type of porcelain developed in the 1840s by a number of potters, and first successfully marketed by Copeland & Garrett who called it porcelain statuary. Wedgwood called their version carrara; and Minton, again with marble in mind, used the term which has stuck, Parian.

The production of Parian figures was made possible by Benjamin Cheverton's 'reducing machine' – no, not a device for weight watchers, but a contrivance which enabled potters to reproduce life-size marble statues, busts and figures exactly to scale in full three-dimensional effect. The machine can still be seen in the Science Museum in London.

As a result of Cheverton's machine, every middle-class household could now have a copy of the famous Canova sculpture *The Three Graces* on their pianoforte. Lady Godiva, a magnificent figure fully 17 inches high, could ride in stately procession across the mantelshelf. And a whole pantheon of classical figures, copied from the original Greek and Roman versions, or the products of contemporary artists working in the Neo-classical style, adorned the parlour, their ivory-hued limbs often protected by a glass dome.

The multiplication of such works of art was initially regarded as an important educational advance, and the fashion for Parian lasted for most of Victoria's reign. Inevitably standards declined, and from being aesthetically instructive works of art Parian production often degenerated into whimsical and sentimental groups of winsome shepherdesses, twee infants, simpering dogs and despairingly drooping maidens.

One type of model remained constant: political and topical heroes. I used to collect political portrait busts. At one time I had over fifty. I rather went off them when a friend complained that he felt uncomfortable in our house 'with all those dead chaps staring at me from the top of the bookcase'.

Parian was big business in Victorian times. It is related that the mountebank sculptor Count d'Orsay offered Herbert Minton a special Duke of Wellington bust in return for a royalty of £1 a head sold. 'When the old Duke dies, then, hey presto, you will make a fortune, Mr Minton.' As he estimated a sale of fifty thousand, Count d'Orsay wasn't doing too badly either. Minton rejected the Count's offer, but his rival W. T. Copeland presumably didn't, for the Copeland model by the Count is dated 1852, the year of the Duke's death. The Duke would sell for three guineas at the most (I doubt if the Count got his £1 royalty) and I paid just £4 for mine in 1960. Now he is worth about £250 which, allowing for inflation since 1852, is still a reasonable price for an excellent likeness of one of our greatest heroes.

THE REVOLUTIONARY PRAYER BOOK

Clive Farahar

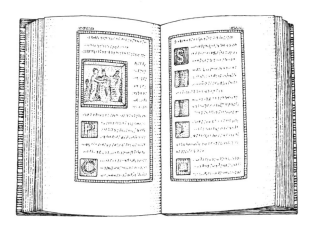

I HAVE ALWAYS ENJOYED book hunting in Portugal. Both Oporto and Lisbon have large expatriate communities, the former centring on the port trade and in Lisbon's case on the deposed royalty of Europe. Their history is redolent with names of voyagers and travellers such as Vasco da Gama and Prince Henry the Navigator. All these influences are reflected in their antiquarian bookshops.

I was routing about in one of the more erudite book stores where I had often found good things. A small red book with a gilt spine and an absence of lettering attracted my attention. As I pulled it out, the bookseller looked up and said, 'Aha, I see you've found it. What do you think?'

It was a small, elegant volume bound in eighteenth-century French leather, with two leather patches on the upper and lower covers where I assumed crests had been. The repairs looked old and were perhaps contemporary, within a year or two of the binding. The book itself was a beautiful manuscript prayer book with a fine broad humanist script and initial letters decorated with burnished gold. 'Well, it's certainly a fine manuscript,' I said as I turned the milky white parchment pages, 'but what a pity about the mutilation of the binding.'

'You are like the French. Unless something is in perfect condition they don't want it. What you have in your hands is an historical relic. Look again and let the scales fall from your eyes. Look at the spine.'

I closed it and gazed at the gilt decorations on the spine. They looked like heraldic fish of some sort, but I couldn't tell what.

'You recognise the Dolphin?' he said.

But I was still mystified. 'Whose crest is the Dolphin?'

'The French for Dolphin, my dear Clive, is . . . '

'Dauphin!' I gasped. 'You mean this belonged to a Dauphin?'

'Exactly – in fact, the unfortunate son of Louis XVI. You may remember about the scandalous behaviour of his jailer, a friend of Marat, who in six months of beatings, kickings and neglect utterly broke the spirit and health of the delicate boy. Despite the jailer's dismissal, the boy spent another six months of absolute neglect without the barest necessities of cleanliness and decency. Later, some better keepers were appointed and they brought a little warmth and brightness into his life. But because of the Royalist reaction in the country, the revolutionary regime was unrelenting. Air, exercise and good food were still denied him. He quickly became ill and, in the arms of his keeper, expired, saying that he could hear heavenly music and the voice of his mother. It cries out as one of the worst crimes of the French Revolution. His jailer stole this, his prayer book, had the crests cut off and then sold it for a few sous.' He paused, and the atmosphere was electric. I looked down again at the exquisite, sad little book that had so much history invested in it. 'I bought it from a French dealer who complained that he couldn't sell it on account of the damaged binding.'

It was a bravura performance and I knew that I had to own this remarkable relic. 'How much? . . . ' I faltered. 'If it is for sale, that is. . . . ' After some preamble about how one could put a price on such a priceless object we settled for what seemed then like an enormous sum of money, and I bore off a great prize to add to my collection.

MONEY IN THE BANK

Hilary Kay

A MEDAL FOR EFFORT should have been presented to the man who tottered into the Tavistock *Roadshow* with a cast-brass cash register. It must have tipped the scales at a couple of hundredweight. This is certainly the largest 'piggy bank' that I have seen at any *Roadshow*. The devices which appear more frequently are smaller cast-iron money banks which have an amusing mechanical action to deposit the coin into safe keeping behind a strong trap door.

The first mechanical cast-iron money banks were produced in America in the 1870s as a profitable sideline for factories usually involved in making domestic and agricultural equipment. The manufacturers took pains to make toys which aptly mirrored or ridiculed contemporary life – national cultural and patriotic figures, domestic scenes, even political scandals and warfare – and the iron banks became an instant success with both children and their parents. The children delighted in the mechanical action which could be quite complex, triggered by a spring or the weight of a coin alone, whilst their parents were equally amused by the hidden connotation of the scene depicted.

A good example is the superficially innocent 'Tammany Bank', first patented in December 1873. In New York in the early 1870s a political storm broke over a politician called William 'Boss' Tweed who was accused of taking bribes from city contractors. The seat of the Democratic Party in New York was called Tammany Hall, and Tweed was one of the 'Tammany' politicians who was tried and subsequently convicted. The iron bank which was inspired by this scandal takes the form of a seated man who slips a proffered coin into his lapel pocket whilst nodding his thanks. Worries over the low morals and questionable lifestyle of the Chinese community at the time were expressed in another bank known as the 'Reclining China-man' bank, which depicts a supine oriental figure holding a poker hand of aces whilst rats run beneath his feet.

According to contemporary reports it would appear that mechanical money banks were not popular in all quarters. In 1898 the *Chicago Tribune* warned that the iron banks 'decoy poor, defenseless little children into dropping their hard-begged for pennies therein to see them work. Some children have been known to cut the bottoms off their Mama's clothes to see the bank do tricks'. Presumably the trimmings could be sold for cash to feed the machines.

In spite of these warnings, cast-iron mechanical banks continued to find favour in the early part of the twentieth century, although their prominence in the market was challenged by banks made in Europe of decorated tinplate. These banks varied a great deal in form and size and were finished in bright hand-painted colours. On some, lithographic printing was used to decorate them in more complex detail. Some of the devices made in Europe took the form of small vend-ing machines: the Stollwerk company in Cologne, for example, made a savings bank which produced miniature bars of chocolate when a coin was deposited, whilst Huntley & Palmers in Reading made one which dispensed their brand of biscuits!

Most collectors of mechanical money banks live in America and it is there that the highest prices have been achieved – as much as $25 000 and $35 000 for particularly scarce examples. Amateur collectors should be careful, though. A large number of modern copies were made in Taiwan in the 1970s and exported widely. Today they are disguised by fifteen years of wear and tear, dust and rust.

TEA THINGS

David Battie

HOT SUMMER DAYS, hot lights, crowds in their thousands. Survival for an expert on *Antiques Roadshow* would be inconceivable without a regular supply of drinks – frequently tea. And without tea, our humble national drink, much of our enviable heritage of works of art would be missing. Collectors of furniture, silver or ceramics would be hard-pressed to build a representative collection without buying a tea-related object. Perhaps one in five pieces brought to the porcelain table at the *Roadshow*, such as the fine famille-Rose tea cannister below, is connected with it.

Tea was originally a medicinal herb, first recorded in use in China in 2700 BC, but not becoming a drink until AD 550. From China its use spread to Japan and India. It appeared in London in the middle of the seventeenth century when tea houses became the centres of discussion and trade. Because of its great expense – over £36 per pound – its use was limited to the wealthy. In 1660 Samual Pepys wrote, 'I did send for a cup of Tee (a China drink) of which I never had drunk before.' The same year a duty of 18 pence was imposed on every gallon of tea made for sale in London.

It is to tea that we owe the large quantities of Chinese, Japanese and Indian works of art imported into Europe from the late seventeenth until the middle of the nineteenth century. The vessels sailing to the East were trading mainly for the precious leaf. The tea was extremely light; porcelain was used as ballast and to raise the tea above the water in the bilges. In some cases it even formed the packing material.

Two types of tea were common, Green and Bohea, and these were kept in the drawing room in a locked tea caddy made of silver, ivory or exotic woods. The hostess would open it with a key kept on her chatelaine* and mix the two teas in the central glass bowl, in proportions to suit her own taste. Using a silver caddy spoon she might transfer the tea to the canister that matched her service, and, in front of the guests, pour the leaves from there into the teapot. Boiling water would be added from the urn standing on its own table to one side. It is a mistaken belief that a tea urn contained tea. It was for hot water, as was the tea kettle on its own stand with spirit burner underneath.

When porcelain was imported into Europe from China – and England imported more than any other country, although much was then re-exported – it was not made up into services. This was done by the wholesaler. Interestingly, far more bowls or cups were imported than saucers, which explains why they are more common today. These cups would be handed round to the guests on a silver salver, as they were for coffee and the far rarer chocolate cups.

When I unceremoniously brew a cuppa with a bag in a mug, I console myself with the thought that when tea was first imported we had little idea of what to do with the leaf – some people even spread it on bread and butter!

---

* Chatelaine – chain of household keys worn by housekeeper or lady of the house.

TEAPOTS ARE HUMAN TOO

Henry Sandon

SEATED ONE DAY at the *Roadshow*, as Sullivan's great song might have put it, I was musing about teapots. As my fingers wandered idly over the obligatory five dozen Japanese 'eggshell' teapots of the 1920s, and then more lovingly over English and European examples, I was struck by the great lost chord.

Do people look like their teapots? I know that people are supposed to look like their dogs, but do they choose the dog because it looks like them, or do they grow to look like their choice of dog? Does that apply to teapots?

At the Guildford *Roadshow*, so much teaware was brought in that I was able to test my theory. There were teapots which were both short and stout and tall and thin. Some were top-heavy, some bottom-heavy, some just round and jolly. There were even eccentric ones with feet and flower-covered bodies, and humorous Art Deco ones of the 1920s in the form of a sports car with the number plate reading T42 – brought in by a Flying Officer Kite type. Most of these pots so resembled their owners that my theory was vindicated.

I had just been teaching my young granddaughter to mime to the little song 'I'm a little teapot, short and stout. Here's my handle, here's my spout. Pick me up and pour me out.' She bends one arm to the hip to represent the handle, and points the other hand to make the spout. Then she bends to pour the tea out.

It reminded me of the one pot that I didn't see at Guildford, the Aesthetic Teapot, made by Royal Worcester in 1881. An example turned up at a London auction house in 1989, and it is my favourite humanised teapot. The teapot, a skit upon the strange Aesthetic Movement and Oscar Wilde, is made in the shape of an Aesthetic young man about town, male on one side

and female on the other. Like the rhyme says, one arm is the handle and the other is the spout, the tea pouring out of the palm. It is coloured in the 'greenery-yallery' colours popularised by the Grosvenor Gallery of London (who were supporters of the Aesthetic Movement) and commemorated in Gilbert and Sullivan's comic opera *Patience*, itself a skit upon the Movement. It pokes fun at an exhibition held in the gallery where a single Japanese teapot was put on display and visitors were invited to contemplate it and go home and 'live up to it'. Under the base is an inscription: 'Fearful consequences through the laws of Natural Selection and Evolution of living up to one's Teapot'.

The Aesthetic Teapot fetched £1500 at the auction and I would love to know what the previous and new owners look like. Let it be a warning that you can grow to look like your teapot – which may not be a bad thing if the teapot is beautiful. Did you see the wonderful Whieldon green-glazed tea or perhaps punch pot that was brought into the Liverpool *Roadshow*? The dear owner's character and cheerful disposition glowed like the pot and I am sure everyone was delighted when she sold it for over £14 000, enabling her to buy her own home. I only hope the new owner receives as much joy from the pot as did its former Liverpudlian owner.

A DELICATE FLUTTER

Penny Brittain

THERE WAS MANY A moment during the long hot summer of 1989 when I would have welcomed the chance to sit quietly behind drawn curtains, fanning myself gently as ladies did in Victorian times. With temperatures soaring to the high nineties when the *Antiques Roadshow* visited Leominster, imagine my delight when I stumbled across a large dress box rustling with tissue paper which, when opened, revealed one person's lifetime passion for collecting fans.

Two hundred years ago the fan was at the peak of its popularity, an accoutrement of high fashion in daily use among society ladies. The dextrous flutter of an open fan could be used to communicate an intimate thought to a potential suitor, whilst adhering to the strict etiquette of the day when chaperones prevented a private conversation or rendez-vous. How much more alluring were a pair of eyes smiling shyly over a beautiful fan painted with a 'Watteauesque' scene of figures relaxing in a fantasy landscape.

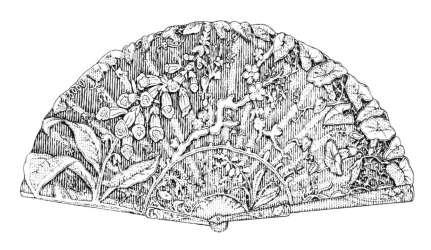

By the end of the seventeenth century France had become the established centre for making fans, but later they were produced throughout Europe as well as being imported from China and Japan. These varied origins reveal themselves in the many different materials used in fans, and in the range of decorative techniques used.

A typical fan has a pleated leaf supported by sticks, with stouter 'guards' at either end to protect the fan when folded. The leaf may be of vellum, paper, silk, lace or, more rarely, of chicken skin. It may be decorated with painting in gouache or watercolour or, as was popular in the late eighteenth century, printed with satirical scenes and homilies. The sticks were often lavishly pierced and carved, sometimes inlaid with silver and occasionally jewel-encrusted. In the early nineteenth century a style of fan became fashionable which dispensed with the leaf altogether, extending beautifully decorated sticks of mother-of-pearl, ivory or horn to form the entire fan. With all this variety from which to choose, ladies could buy exactly the right fan to suit any occasion, constrained only by the privy purse.

It is their individuality and diversity that makes fans so popular with collectors today. Opportunities still exist to buy fans at reasonable prices, both at auction and from antique shops and fairs. Examples from the eighteenth century and earlier are rarer and inevitably more costly, with a good example commanding £500–800, but there are many less expensive fans to be found. Most frequently seen on the market are those dating from the end of the nineteenth century and the early twentieth century – often marvellously elaborate in lace and ostrich feathers. It is most important for collectors to check the condition of any fan they consider – aim to buy only perfect examples, because restoration can be costly. Likewise, it is important to look after fans properly to preserve them. Sadly this means the less fluttering the better. Perhaps I had better rely on the air-conditioning after all if we ever again have a summer like 1989.

STRIKE A LIGHT

Ian Pickford

IF ANYONE WAS TO say to you that the modern cigarette lighter owed its origins to George III snuff boxes, you would probably be a bit sceptical. So how did this curious transformation take place?

Vestas were wax matches with red phosphorus tops ignited by friction. They were first produced in the 1830s and replaced the earlier, more cumbersome and more difficult-to-use tinder boxes. Existing snuff boxes were modified to carry these vestas, with the addition of a striking plate to the side or base.

By the 1840s these 'snuff-box'-style vesta cases were being made in small numbers, mostly in London. They were, however, by no means popular – probably owing to the fact that there were some nasty accidents with people setting fire to themselves. The main problem lay in the design. When the lid was opened it exposed the greatest possible area. The solution was found in the 1850s by making what had been the side of the box into the lid, thus retaining the capacity but reducing the exposed area when opened. This, of course, diminished the chance of accidental ignition. With the added refinements of an interior spring (so that the lid snapped shut and would not open accidentally), together with the rounding of the corners to stop holes being worn in pockets, the vesta case in its most recognisable and common form was born.

By the end of the nineteenth century this standard form must have been made in Birmingham by the tens of thousands, a good many of which we see on the *Roadshow*. Sometimes the decoration on a standard form of case can increase the value quite considerably. A case enamelled as a pack of playing cards would be about ten times the price of a plain one. Naked women can be much more!

Apart from the standard examples, a wide range of novelty

shapes were produced. A very rare one that turned up on an *Antiques Roadshow* was in the form of a violin case. Although it was only electroplated, it was still worth about £200. The most amusing must be the model of a wooden privy which when opened reveals an enthroned gentleman wearing a top hat and a smile.

The most valuable to date must be the rare and very fine fisherman's creel which was sold for £1750. At the other end of the scale are the base metal advertising examples which were virtually handed out with the cornflakes! Often poorly made, many of these can be picked up for a few pounds. They are none the less very collectable because of the wide range of advertisers involved – from high street tailors to biscuit manufacturers.

But how do we progress from this to the petrol lighter? The idea for lighters was developed at the time of the First World War by the French who fitted the lighter mechanism into existing vesta cases. These were very popular with the troops and spread rapidly through the trenches, soon finding their way back to England. The vesta case was replaced almost overnight.

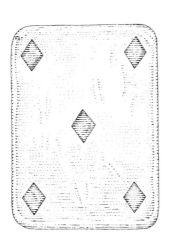

THE ART DECO YEARS

Eric Knowles

WHEN THE CHIMES OF Big Ben heralded the arrival of 1920 the new decade was greeted with hope and optimism for a peaceful future, free from the horrors and misery experienced during the war years of 1914-18. Today the 'Roaring Twenties' are synonymous with jazz music, cocktail parties and dance crazes such as the charleston and the black bottom, not forgetting the gangster underworld of speakeasies and bootleg liquor in America. In the realm of decorative arts the most significant event was the Exposition des Arts Décoratifs held in Paris during 1925, and from which the term Art Deco is derived.

For some time I believed that the twenties represented the golden years of Art Deco, and that what followed during the thirties was little more than a rehash of themes popularised in the previous decade. But with the benefit of research I must now admit to being wrong. The two decades are inextricably linked as a result of the latter commencing before the former had fully expired. To be more precise, 1930 might be said to have arrived on 25 October 1929 – the day of the Wall Street Crash.

The decade of the thirties invokes for many of us images of the depression that shook Europe and America alike. Yet in the world of design and decorative arts there was little to depress and much to applaud. Those designers catering for the luxury market continued to provide a service for the financially sound elite, with Paris reigning as the centre of refined taste in interior design. Think of names like Ruhlmann, Lalique and Dunand.

It has taken almost fifty years for the British to recognise that the monopoly in good design in this period did not belong entirely to the French. Back home in Blighty the thirties produced a wealth of designers whose names appear today in the catalogues of prestigious West End galleries and premier auction houses.

In ceramic design Clarice Cliff is presently enjoying unprecedented popularity, with her rarer pottery achieving prices that match her trade name, Bizarre. Susie Cooper cannot be ignored, although for some inexplicable reason her ceramic designs have not aroused the same interest and following enjoyed by Clarice Cliff. The New Zealand-born designer Keith Murray designed a whole range of distinctive geometric-form vases and useful wares for Wedgwood, which at the beginning of the 1990s have begun to rise steeply in price. The company also commissioned designs from the artist Eric Ravilious, and the popularity of these is beginning to match in price those of John Flaxman who was employed by Wedgwood some 150 years earlier. Furniture of the period designed and retailed by Gordon Russell, Betty Joel and Heal's is limited in appeal today, often because of its sheer size. Bedroom furniture, which often used woodgrain as the main decorative feature, was particularly large.

The decade that arrived early disappeared into the war clouds of 1939, taking with it the Art Deco years. And from the six hard years of hostilities that followed there emerged a new approach labelled 'Utility'. Now there's an idea for a new collection.

LEIGHTON'S LAZY LAD

Christopher Payne

IN 1846 THE POET BEAUDELAIRE wrote a review of the Paris Salon under the title 'Why Sculpture Is Boring'. The Salon was an annual exhibition of painting and sculpture; the aim of the latter was to show new ideas and ideals in the art of modelling. Often exhibits would be in terracotta or plaster. Viewers could then commission a version in bronze from the sculptor, if they wished. Like their fellow artists in paint, impoverished sculptors could often not afford to make a bronze cast without a patron who would provide the money 'up front'.

Beaudelaire's point was that sculpture had become a stale pastiche of the Classical style of the eighteenth century. The time was ripe for change. By the 1860s French sculptors were applying dramatic sculptural features to buildings in Paris such as the Opéra by Carpeaux. However, it was in England that a New School of Sculpture evolved. It wasn't an academic institution which started it but a peer of the realm, who in 1876 produced the dramatic figure of *Athlete Wrestling with a Python*. A critic described it as 'something wholly new, propounded by a painter . . . '. This was the beginning of the English New School.

This painter-turned-sculptor was Lord Frederick Leighton. He was in the same school of sculpture as Sir Alfred Gilbert, the creator of the Shaftesbury Memorial – Eros in Piccadilly Circus. The movement of which they were members flourished around the turn of the century, in late Victorian and Edwardian England.

One of 'Fred's' most famous works, and arguably his best, was his nude figure of *The Sluggard*. This slim youth is modelled in all his glory, standing and yawning lazily, stretching his arms above his head in a manner so languid that it makes us jealous that he has so much time, indeed eternity, in which to wake up. It must have been a Sunday morning for Fred to have captured such a mood with his portrait of the young Italian Giuseppe Valona.

Imagine my surprise and delight when, almost at the end of a blustery day in Hastings on the *Antiques Roadshow*, a *Sluggard* appeared with his arms sticking out of someone's paper bag. Heart quickening, I strode with Battie-like eagerness to claim the prize. (My colleague David Battie is well known for being fast off the mark when he thinks he's spied something really good, elbowing others out of the way.) 'That might be for me,' I suggested, trying to sound calm and unconcerned. The poor owner had not even had time to present himself at the reception desk.

Would it be a false alarm – another of those commercially produced French dancing girls which were so popular at the time? Would it be made of cheap spelter, rather than bronze? I examined it carefully. 'It could be interesting,' I said nonchalantly, feeling rather like a knocker* about to make the deal of the century. It was perfect, and its owner had not the slightest notion of its value. 'What do you think it's worth?' I asked as I reached the climax of the recording.

'Er – possibly £500?' he suggested nervously.

I smiled. The value? Around £10000. If you want to see *The Sluggard*, Liverpool University Art Gallery has just acquired one with the help of the National Art Collections Fund.

* Knocker – itinerant dealer who calls on householders without invitation.

A LITTLE
DAMP SALT

Michael Clayton

IN THE PORTOBELLO ROAD the other day I bought a very nice heavy silver salt cellar, hallmarked 1745, for £65, and a pair of salt spoons for another £30. It always seems strange that single salt cellars, however nice, fetch so much less than a pair. In the eighteenth century they were usually sold in sets of four.

My salt cellar reminded me of an occasion years ago when I was summoned to a client in Norfolk. I left London at about half-past six on a brilliant summer's morning, my directions being to 'go to Norwich, bear right and we are not far from such and such Broad, then ask . . . '. By eleven o'clock I was deep in the lanes, miles from anywhere. By pure chance I saw a peeling signboard bearing the name of the house I was looking for. I followed the drive through the woods until suddenly I arrived in a clearing with the house on one side and water beyond – a marvellous spot.

I rang the bell. Nothing happened. I went in, but there was nobody about. When I came out, an elderly man was standing beside my car. I thought he might have been the gardener, but since the place was a complete wilderness I decided it must be my client. He had totally forgotten that I was expected.

The house was filthy. The silver, mostly spoons, forks and some silver-handled knives, was scattered in various cupboards and drawers, and it was all by Paul de Lamerie, the greatest of the eighteenth-century silversmiths. As I kept oohing and aahing, the old man kept producing more.

By now it was early afternoon, and the last thing I had had to eat was breakfast before I started. So when he suggested something for lunch, I accepted with alacrity. He disappeared into the back regions to return with two plates, a tin of steak and kidney pudding and a tin opener with which he proceeded to open the tin and divide the contents between us, stone cold. I selected one of the less tarnished Lamerie forks and we started to eat, until he suddenly said, 'Oh, we need some salt.' He disappeared again, and returned with a salt cellar – which I knew the moment I saw it was also going to be by Lamerie. I asked if there were any more salts. 'Oh, yes,' he said, 'two or three'. There was indeed a set of four.

They were absolutely black inside and out, the result of years of neglect. They had been left filled with salt in a damp house. When they were new they would have had gilded linings to protect the silver from the action of the salt, but it had long since been scoured away.

Eventually I left to drive back to London with all the Lamerie silver in the back of the car. The following day, before having the salt cellars photographed with a view to illustrating them in the sale catalogue, I tried to clean them. Nothing happened. So I resorted to boiling them in an aluminium pan with a piece of freshly scraped aluminium and soda in the hope that this would have more effect. They turned from black to grey but still looked more like pewter, and they had to be sold in that condition. Long afterwards I saw them sitting in a museum showcase, but even the resources of the museum laboratory had failed to remove the years of damp amongst the Broads.

EVEN A COPY CAN BE COLLECTABLE

Paul Hollis

A CEREMONIAL SPADE, commemorating the inauguration of a new sewage works, turned up at the Blackpool *Antiques Roadshow*. It was a fine example of the work of the hugely successful firm of Elkington, which dominated the nineteenth-century silver and plate business.

The firm was run in partnership by two cousins, George Richards Elkington (1801–65) and Henry Elkington (1810–52), and in 1840 they patented the process of electro-plating. Electro-plating is the method by which base metal, normally copper or nickel, is silver-plated by submerging the base metal article in a vat of electrolyte (any liquid that conducts electricity) through which an electric current is passed causing pure silver to adhere to the object.

Although experiments had been carried out in the early part of the nineteenth century, Elkington were the first company with the foresight to capitalise on such a revolutionary process. Until then the only commercial process employed in the plating industry was what we know as Old Sheffield Plate, first developed in the late 1740s. This was a technique in which a sandwich of copper and silver was rolled out in sheet form to be fashioned in the same way as sterling silver. The chief commercial difference between Old Sheffield Plate and electro-plate was the huge saving of labour, making the latter finished product available to 'all classes', an ideal of the nineteenth century.

Having obtained the decisive patent for electro-plating the Elkingtons began to expand their business, purchasing existing patents for the new process and then licensing other British and Continental manufacturers, thus maintaining a grip of iron on the new process. So successful did they become that they established their own date letter cycle, which makes it possible to tell the actual date when a particular piece was manufactured. Although the company did not stamp every article, it is a measure of their success that today we can tell the exact date not only of their silver – a statutory hallmark requirement – but also of a large proportion of their lesser-value electro-plate.

Electro-plate was by no means the only triumph of the company. Apart from major works in silver, Elkington pioneered the process known as electrotyping, a related method in which, having obtained a master pattern or model, a number of silver or plated copies could be electroformed without the labour-intensive skills associated with the silversmith. The Ladies' All England Lawn Tennis and Croquet Club Trophy, raised aloft by so many distinguished players at Wimbledon, is an Elkington electrotype of a pewter salver by Caspar Enderlein in the Louvre.

The firm of Elkington epitomised the pioneering spirit of nineteenth-century manufacturing, where art and science were joined in a glorious testimonial to an increasingly prosperous and confident nation. Today, with the shortage of fine and rare silver, electro-plate by Elkington, such as the 1853 tureen illustrated below, is collected in its own right and I am sure will be more so in the future.

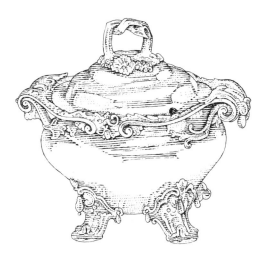

BULLETS, BLADE AND KNUCKLE-SANDWICH!

Bill Harriman

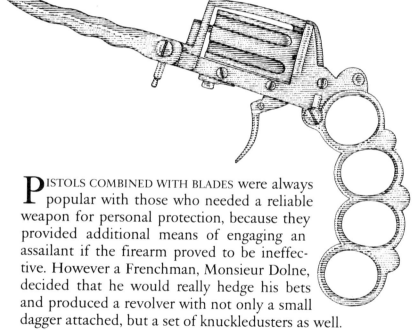

PISTOLS COMBINED WITH BLADES were always popular with those who needed a reliable weapon for personal protection, because they provided additional means of engaging an assailant if the firearm proved to be ineffective. However a Frenchman, Monsieur Dolne, decided that he would really hedge his bets and produced a revolver with not only a small dagger attached, but a set of knuckledusters as well. These bizarre-looking weapons were mainly manufactured in France and Belgium between *c.*1870 and 1895 and are referred to as Apache pistols by collectors – not after the Indians of North America, but after the hoodlums who terrorised Paris at this period. This attribution has no real historical substance, and the only contemporary reference to these weapons that I have been able to find was in the American *Sporting Goods Gazette* for November 1889. It was reported that

Policeman Hastings brought Captain Eugene Arbrille
of the steamship *Runnymeade*, to the Jefferson Market
Court, New York, and with him one of the most
remarkable deadly weapons ever seen in this country.
The weapon is a combination of brass knuckles, horse
pistol and dagger, and is fully a foot in length. The
officer saw the seaman draw it on a man in West
Third Street.

The captain was detained and eventually fined $100, a large
sum in those days.

The heart of this weapon is a 5mm pinfire revolver in which
the cartridges have small pins protruding from their sides,
which fire when struck by the hammer. Instead of a barrel, it
has an elongated six-shot cylinder which rotates around a central axis. The hammer is self-cocking and all six shots could be
fired in under two seconds, though reloading was fiddly and
probably took a minute or so. The wavy-edged dagger blade is
made ready for action by turning it through 180° until it locks
in place by means of a small spring catch. The knuckleduster,
which doubles as a grip for the revolver, can only be used when
the weapon is folded away.

Over the 1980s such weapons, which are classed as 'Curiosa'
by gun collectors, have risen steadily in value. My pistol would
now command between £300 and £350 at auction. An additional advantage is that no licence is required to own them, as
they are subject to neither the Firearms Act 1968/1988 nor the
Criminal Justice Act 1988, from which offensive weapons
dating from pre-1900 are excluded. Beware, though, for con-
vincing modern forgeries are becoming common.

Despite its fearsome appearance, the Apache pistol would
not have been very effective. The tiny 5mm bullets would be
easily deflected by substantial clothing. The dagger is flimsy
and too short. Of the trio, the knuckleduster is by far the most
useful weapon. However, in purely psychological terms the
device must have been terrifying to those confronted by it.

LITTLE BOYS LIKE DOLLS TOO

Bunny Campione

I WAS AMUSED TO BE SHOWN a French doll during the *Roadshow* in Leeds. Her wig had been cut by the owner when she was a child. It reminded me of many dolls brought to me in the past – miserable apparitions whose wigs had been mutilated and chopped into jagged points or crew-cuts.

Although some dolls were manufactured as boys with short-cropped hair and boys' clothes – but with no anatomical features that I'm aware of – it is quite logical for a child to cut its doll's wig and expect it to grow again, just as it is to expect the doll to become cleaner by washing and scrubbing it with soap in the bath. It probably does – but imagine the distress when the elastic stringing which holds the doll together snaps and a sinister assortment of arms, legs and ball joints floats to the surface of the water, the eyes staring menacingly up from the murky depths. What a horror to lift out a peeling torso and retrieve the bedraggled remains of your beloved Rosebud or Rosalie!

In the nineteenth and early twentieth centuries few children were lucky enough to have a doll, and fewer still had a nanny to ensure the doll stayed in one piece. Among the limbless torsos and crew-cut hairstyles which survived you would think there was little of value left, but you'd be wrong. Even a bodyless, eyeless, limbless bisque head can be worth thousands of pounds if it is a rare mould number or make, so long as it has no cracks or blemishes. The rarest Kämmer and Reinhardt head, mould number 105, can make £20 000 plus with no body at all. A Bru bisque head can make up to £6000, depending on size.

It is generally accepted that girls are gentler with their toys than boys. Maybe it is only that boys are taught at an early age to be tough and manly, although several men friends have admitted to me that they preferred dolls to tin toys.

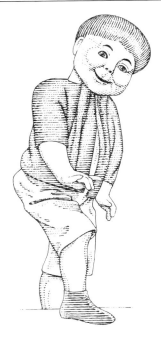

One of these men friends was the fifth of five sons. His mother, on discovering her much longed for daughter was yet another boy, became so distraught in her disappointment that she determined to ignore the all-too-apparent truth. She forthwith clothed him in skirts and dresses, refused to cut his hair, called him Matilda and taught him how to play with her grandmother's dolls. I am not quite sure exactly what this entailed, but under normal circumstances a boy would drag a doll about by its biceps, hair or feet as Sebastian Flyte did his teddy bear Aloysius in *Brideshead Revisited*. Not so Matilda, who treated his dolls with loving care. I never heard what Matilda's father had to say on the matter.

By the age of fourteen Matilda's voice was breaking and his mother finally had to acknowedge his gender. He was renamed Matt and allowed to wear trousers and go to a boys' school. His dolls were packed up and put away and he rapidly discovered the vastly preferable merits of the real thing – girls.

The end of my story is that Matt married and produced – boys. His doll collection went up for auction and realised a small fortune – over £50 000, and that was several years ago. How lucky that he was taught to play so gently with his dolls!